'Great nuggets on how to convert marketing insights into business results!'

**Sanjay Khosla**
*Senior Fellow, Kellogg School of Management,*
*Northwestern University*
*Former President, Kraft Foods International*

'...full of wisdom, deep and clarifying, and packed with real-life examples. It is beautifully written, in simple, uncluttered prose that slices through the noise around the subject of integrated marketing. A book with a clear perspective that is both provocative and enlightening; it is a must-read for practitioners, students and for anyone even slightly interested in marketing.'

**Santosh Desai**
*CEO, Futurebrands*

'Chintamani Rao truly understands the intricacies of integrated marketing. Drawing upon a wealth of professional experience, he presents a refreshingly straightforward perspective on how to cut through the maze of complexity to create the most effective communications solutions.'

**Sheila Byfield**
*Communications and Research Consultant*
*Former Global Director, Insights, Mindshare*

'Chintamani's insights into a number of Indian brands should stimulate a healthy debate. This well-written book is rooted in the recent past and he refrains from making speculations about the future.'

**John Philip Jones**

*Emeritus Professor, Newhouse School of Public Communications, Syracuse University*

'Rao's succinct analysis of how to apply the wisdom of experience to today's complex marketing. It is a must-read.'

**Hap Klopp**

*Founder, The North Face*

'Laced with examples, rich in anecdotes, enlivened with cases... all with an underlying concern that marketing music deserves to be played with aplomb. This book is a timely reminder to all professionals that the fragmentation in the marketing services domain needs to be addressed and pulled back for it to deliver to its potential. If you are in the business, don't miss reading this.'

**Shekar Swamy**

*CEO, R K Swamy BBDO*

'*Making Marketing Music* is a compelling read for those interested in why and how the industry got to where it is today. Chinta, as only he can, takes a broad, long-term and strategic view of the forces that have driven the industry and the consequences it has endured. He cuts through the buzzword banalities and shows us, with several brilliant examples from his own work, what great marketing looks like. Most importantly, though, the value of this book lies in reminding us that marketing is about people, and little else matters.'

**Shekhar Deshpande**
*Head of Strategy, Global Accounts, Facebook*

'Chinta's book underlines the importance of basics while simultaneously underlining the need to understand and embrace the changing environment. The India-specific cases make the book a must-read for all in the overall communication ecosystem, not just those in advertising and marketing.'

**Anant Rangaswami**
*Editor, MELT*
*Former Editor, Storyboard*
*Founder Editor, Campaign India*

# Making Marketing Music

# Making Marketing Music

## Integrated Marketing Communications at Work

Chintamani Rao

BLOOMSBURY
NEW DELHI • LONDON • OXFORD • NEW YORK • SYDNEY

BLOOMSBURY INDIA
Bloomsbury Publishing India Pvt. Ltd
Second Floor, LSC Building No. 4, DDA Complex, Pocket C – 6 & 7,
Vasant Kunj, New Delhi 110070

BLOOMSBURY, BLOOMSBURY INDIA and the Diana logo are trademarks of Bloomsbury Publishing Plc

First published in India 2019
This export edition published in 2020



ISBN:PB: 978-93-88271-72-1; eBook: 978-9-3882-7173-8

Typeset in Manipal Digital

# To the Mad Men

In spending the largest part of my career in the advertising business, I have had the good fortune to have known and worked with some of the giants of Indian advertising, those who shaped the advertising industry in the country—the original Mad Men of India. Each left his imprint on the industry; each nurtured later leaders of the business; and each enriched my life.

I learnt different things from them: from a passion for consumer knowledge to an understanding of industry issues; from brand strategy to people management; from a sense of history to a sense of drama; from mentoring to financial management. And what I got from all of them was their infectious passion for the profession.

To the memory of these great men, in admiration and in gratitude for what they gave me, this book is humbly dedicated. They are (in order of their appearance in my life):

Subroto Sen Gupta

R K Swamy

Subhas Ghosal

Alyque Padamsee

Mani Ayer

Ranjan Kapur

# Contents

# Preface

When traditional advertising agencies first added communication skills beyond advertising, some coined a label or a description for their new, wider communications offering. Ogilvy & Mather called theirs Ogilvy Orchestration, bringing together the agency's 'many instruments and voices to form one big sound'.

The analogy with an orchestra is most apt. The music we hear is a composite whole, made up of sounds of different instruments. They don't all make the same sound at the same time, but their collective sound moves us. To produce that effect, an orchestra performs to a musical score under the direction of a conductor. That is how marketing communications must work. When we assemble our communications instruments and conduct them effectively, we make marketing music.

The problem with integrated marketing communications now is that every player in the orchestra wants to be a soloist, and the resulting sound is often a cacophony. It is no longer a concept or a way of thinking; it is just a term. IMC, for short, or 360, as in, 'We should do IMC,' or, 'We want a 360 plan'.

Once upon a time, it was just something we did. Now we have a term for what we used to do, and instead of practising it we lament that we don't, and have seminars about its whys and wherefores.

When I was a young Account Director in an advertising agency we were once doing completely new advertising to revive an old brand and I thought, in a simplistic way, it would be nice if there were some write-ups about it in the magazines. When the client said they didn't have the budget to pay a public relations agency, I suggested they cut a few spots off the TV schedule and use that money, which they did. It happened across the table: no presentation, no big deal. No one told me that was something called IMC. (And my bosses didn't chastise me for giving up some billing.)

When Philips launched epilators, we thought a woman who wasn't familiar with the product couldn't possibly buy one without trying it. But how could she try one in a shop? So the ads offered a free in-home demo. A demo cost three times as much as the product, but the customer invariably invited others over; so each demo reached several women, a nice girlie time was had by all, and the demos seeded the product in a virgin market. Of course, we also had in-shop product detailing and got the product featured in appropriate magazine columns. We did this because we thought our job was to get the product in the woman's hand, not just to make ads. No one told us this was 360° communication.

When Toyota launched the Corona in Indonesia, Ogilvy was assigned the Direct Marketing account. We knew that our best prospects were satisfied Toyota Corolla upgraders, and we knew that the average car replacement cycle was three years. As we sat around a table batting thoughts around, in typical agency style, an idea began to take shape. Toyota's local partner, Astra, also owned Auto 2000, the largest auto retail chain in the country; Mobil 88, a used car dealership; and Astra Finance, a finance company that gave auto loans. Put this together, and what do you have?

We identified those who had owned a Toyota Corolla for two years or more, and then here's what happened. Against the backdrop of the on-going advertising of all the businesses, including that for the new Toyota Corona, this Corolla owner received an invitation from Auto 2000 to test drive the new car. Meanwhile, he also got a mailer from Mobil 88 telling him that there was a good market for two- to three-year-old Corollas and inviting him to drive in for a free valuation. About the same time he got a mailer from Astra Finance, offering finance for the Toyota Corona on attractive terms. So, in three seemingly independent but orchestrated pieces of targeted communication, the hot prospect was invited to experience the new car, offered assistance to buy it and offered help to dispose of his old car. Loop closed.

When we worked this out, there was no great flash of brilliance, no thunder and lightning. No one told us it was IMC or a 360° plan. It just seemed like a good idea—even a clever little idea—and a lot of hard work ahead, given the limited data processing capabilities of the time.

Once upon a time, advertising agencies and their ilk were in the business of inducing consumers to do something. Now, we are in the business of making ads, or buying media, putting out mailers, managing social media, or wearing whichever hat life has placed on our heads. It is no one's job but the marketer's to focus on the end result. We know IMC—or 360, take your pick—is a good thing, so we talk about it and regret that we don't do what we know we should.

On the one hand, advertisers feel free to shop ad hoc for bits and pieces of their marketing communications needs, some of them work with thousands of shops around the world and even business leaders like Unilever resort to crowdsourcing. On the other hand, agency holding companies—WPP Group, Interpublic Group (IPG), etc.—stitch together, time and again, dedicated multidiscipline units, drawn out of their specialist shops, to service large global clients. They have had limited success and the jury is still out on whether such units are the solution.

So what's the problem with the term? It's not the specific term; it's the descent into jargon, which often gives the illusion of thinking. We used to think of the consumer. Now we say we must do IMC, or 360, and ask what we should do in social media, and so on, so we can tick off the boxes.

The good news is that we in India aren't the only ones who do that; it's the same globally. The bad news is that we in India aren't the only ones who do that; it's the same globally. Just how mindless it can be came home to me a long time ago, when I saw a TV interview with Trevor Beattie, former Chairman and Creative Director of TBWA, London.

When asked about integrated marketing communications, Beattie said it wasn't about just ticking boxes. So far, so good. He said what mattered was the quality of each thing you did. Oh, so now we know. If you do everything well, that's integrated marketing communications. But wait, there's more to it. He said it's the tone of voice that matters. And to illustrate, he gave the example of his agency's work for FCUK in which, he said, the TV commercial, the posters, the store displays and whatever else had exactly the same tone of voice. So what we learn from him is that you must tick all the boxes with the same colour.

It's not that anything Beattie said was wrong; it's that he missed the point. Typically, he was thinking of what *we* do; he was not thinking of *what we want the consumer to do; how we can nudge them to do it; what comes in the way of their doing it; and what we need to do about that.* That is what marketing communications, and indeed the very concept of marketing, is about: them, not us. We think of the tools, and try to use as many of them as we can. We need to think instead about what we want to build, and use the tools needed to build it.

Much of what I describe in this book happened a long time ago, but you will find the situations and the issues equally familiar today. I have chosen the examples and stories I have because they clearly illustrate the underlying principles of marketing communications. In fact, the advantage of looking at what happened a long way back is that of detached observation: no one has an emotional stake in it, which makes it easier to see what it illustrates instead of getting caught up in the minutiae of it.

# CHAPTER 1
# A Crisis of Faith

**'Future historians of our trade will be baffled. Towards the end of the 20th century more and more marketing companies were converted to a belief in seamless, all-media, 360°, harmonised, orchestrated, integrated communications. And at exactly the same time the purveyors of those communications disintegrated completely.**

**...So why, historians will wonder, was client demand for integrated communications met, paradoxically, by supplier fragmentation?'**

***—Jeremy Bullmore***
*'Who's going to sit at the client's top table?'*
*Admap, October 2004*

Consider the business director of a big, important client's account in an advertising agency. He believes one of the client's brands needs communication support beyond advertising. If he brings in one or more other divisions of the agency, he runs into the following risks:

1. He loses part of his 'rightful' revenue to other divisions
2. Other divisions have conflicting commitments and don't want to handle the business
3. Other divisions don't find the business large or profitable enough for senior level attention

4. He doesn't like their work but has to defend it because they belong to the same agency
5. Other divisions don't deliver, and he is left to handle a disgruntled client

In any event, he is not evaluated or rewarded for other divisions' business.

If, on the other hand, he leaves the client to find and implement their own solutions, he runs none of these risks and can focus on his own deliverables.

What is he likely to do?

In the last twenty years, every significant advertising agency has set up or acquired specialist divisions for direct marketing, public relations, design, promotions, etc.

These divisions have been caught in a conflict: to be and to deliver as part of an integrated agency team they have to respond to a common rallying cry, but to be taken seriously as practitioners of their disciplines, they must have their own identity and reputation.

In addition to that, each is a profit centre with its own P&L imperative and its own independent clients to deliver to. 'Integrated' clients expect priority service—at a special price because they are clients across disciplines—but are often priority only to the division that brought them in, in the first place.

## In the Beginning...

Not so long ago, the advertising agency was the client's marketing advisor. A full-service agency would do a market analysis, make a business plan, a marketing plan, a communication strategy and plan, a media plan—and oh, of course, create the ads as well as packaging, and point-of-sale merchandising material, and throw in thoughts and ideas on sales promotion, PR or direct marketing too. So the client would get integrated communications advice without the term ever being used—and all for free with the ads, for which the agency was paid a 15% commission on the money the client spent to place those ads in the media.

It was a strange business model, in which the advertising agency was paid for buying media, but the cost of providing the value-added services—from research and account planning to creating and producing the ads, and media planning—was far greater than that of media-buying services.

In fact, the very origin of advertising agencies was as media buyers, as agents who earned a commission to go out and procure ads for newspaper publishers.[1] As all agents were competing to sell the same white space (that was before TV), the differentiator was the service. Over time, the value addition of creating the ads to fill the white space became the essential service that made one agent different from another—and so the modern advertising agency was born. Perhaps the only agent whose name lives on is J Walter Thompson (even if the agency has recently morphed into Wunderman Thompson).

Despite all the evolution of business in the following hundred years and more, that mindset did not change. The agency continued to be paid for media buying and for providing the ads to place in the media it bought. Growing up with the commission system, the agencies developed a vested interest—even if unstated, or even subconscious—in how much their clients spent on mass media. Even the best of clients are often faintly suspicious of their agency's intentions when it suggests that a troubled or threatened brand needs more advertising.

A landmark event was the creation of the Account Planning function. In 1968 Stephen King at JWT and Stanley Pollitt at Boase Massimi Pollitt, both in London, started it independently of each

1 'Agency' is really a euphemism for the crass 'agent'. Even today, the advertising industry body in Hong Kong is called the Association of Accredited Advertising Agents, not 'Agencies'.

other, to bring an informed basis to the creation of advertising. That was probably the biggest step in the modernisation of advertising.

It was in the 1980s that the advertising industry began to notice what it saw as a shift of marketing budgets from mass media advertising to sales promotion, direct marketing, public relations, and the like. It was not so much a shift—because advertising spending too was growing—as that incremental marketing spends were going more and more into activities other than mass media advertising, which continued to be the agencies' staple.

As marketing expenditures began to diversify the agencies saw lost revenue, on the one hand, and a business opportunity, on the other. It was only natural for them to start offering specialist services in other disciplines like direct marketing, sales promotion and public relations. The agency could, thus, remain true to the brand and offer unbiased advice and then go on to implement the solutions through its specialist services.

One part of the problem, however, was that clients did not see it that way. Many did not see this as holistic problem solving by a fully equipped communications partner. They saw it instead as their agency diversifying and then drumming up business for its divisions, which in that relationship was infra dig. Those who did appreciate the agency's initiative and understood the need for orchestrated, multidiscipline communications were not necessarily convinced that their agency was the best in class. They bought the idea but not the one-stop shop offer and went out and shopped for each service.

The other part of the problem was in the way agencies structured the business and indeed continue to. Each specialisation was set up as a division with its own revenue, profit and client responsibilities and was encouraged to go out and seek its own business and independent existence. That made good business logic, but no one in the system was rewarded for driving client business across disciplines, so no one did.

For long second-class citizens in small 'cells' within the agency, specialists now found their place in the sun and guarded it jealously. So graphic designers, packaging designers, direct marketing people, public relations people, all thrived in their own specialist units. Many of those who started out in newly created divisions of advertising agencies then went out and set up their own companies. Later, many of these were acquired by advertising agency holding companies looking to quickly strengthen their offering in one discipline or another!

Meanwhile, another huge change was taking place. Until the late 1980s advertising agencies, even the large international ones, were relatively small shops, mostly privately owned and run by people with a passion. Business was simple; you did what you had to do and made a little money in the process. Shares of the few agencies that were listed on the stock exchange were little traded, held mostly by friendly investors or by stable, long-term investors like pension funds. Interpublic Group (IPG), the original advertising agency holding company, was relatively unknown outside the financial market; only its powerful brands, like McCann-Erickson, were.

The change probably started with Saatchi & Saatchi, which went about acquiring advertising agencies at such a pace that industry wags said 'SAATCHI' was an acronym for 'Single Advertising Agency Takes Control of Half the Industry'. Saatchi's Finance Director, Martin Sorrell, quit to start doing the same for himself and created WPP, and built it into the world's biggest and arguably most powerful marketing services conglomerate. (He has since quit WPP and started another new network.) With rapid acquisitions and mergers, advertising agencies became part of multi-billion-dollar conglomerates listed on the stock exchanges in New York, London and Paris. Along the way, all kinds of specialist companies too got swept in: direct marketing, public relations, graphic design, corporate identity, internal communications, web design, digital specialists, data analytics, etc.

What this development did was to change forever the essential character of the advertising agency. From being simple client-centric services, even if with an international presence, they became large, complex companies, answerable to the stock markets or at least to holding companies that were answerable to the stock markets. No longer were advertising agencies driven by client needs and fired by passion. They were driven by quarterly financial results and—at least at the very top—fired by stock prices.

Through this upheaval, the advertising agency's compensation model remained unchanged: the legendary 15% commission continued to be how it earned its money! At the top were the holding companies, each of which owned several advertising agencies. Before long, the accountants saw an opportunity. If the holding company consolidated the media buying of all its advertising agencies under one roof, it could create a single 800-pound gorilla that could go stomping around the media houses, buy media cheaper for its clients, and so add another competitive advantage to its arsenal.

WPP Group's Mindshare was perhaps first off the block. With further mergers and acquisitions and to handle competing businesses, each holding company now has several media agencies and, with a second level merger, WPP's media agencies are consolidated into Group M and IPG's into Mediabrands.

What this development did was to take not only media buying but, in the process, media planning too out of the advertising agency. The media planner brought the market perspective to the business: where are the client's markets? North or south? Metro or small town? What do they watch and read? So what is the best way to reach them? Where is the competition advertising: in which markets, in which media? How much pressure are they putting on? Without this perspective the advertising agency shoots in the dark: it just creates ads, with no idea about when and where they will run. Worse, it does not even know which media make for the best use of the client's money.

Meanwhile, media agencies increasingly focused on buying cheap: media strategy and planning became secondary. This is not really surprising, since consolidating volume to buy cheap was why they came into existence in the first place.

So the advertising agency, once the client's closest strategic advisor, has reduced itself to a maker of ads. Its seat at the top table has been taken by, if anyone, the media agency, wearing its buyer hat and telling cost-pressured clients how much money it has saved them. If anyone in the agency does get invited to the corner office, it is the creative head. More and more in recent years, the creative heads of agencies are dealing directly with clients, presenting and selling ideas. The evidence of that, certainly in India, is in the fact that most of the top advertising agencies are headed by their creative chiefs, which is in fact entirely in keeping with the narrower role of the agency.

Of course, this does not mean marketers are not communicating nearly as much as they used to, or are not using multiple channels of communication. It only means that they are doing so on their own, without taking the advertising agency into confidence.

Meanwhile, the average person's media repertoire has not only diversified but also become increasingly complex. As marketers and agencies were wrapping their heads around digital media, along came smartphones, and people began carrying the internet in their pocket, engaging with it several times a day, even while watching TV. The advent and growth of social media further compounded the situation.

Much of this makes intuitive sense or is the behaviour most of us have observed. To connect the dots, though, and design communication based on the picture that emerges is the job of the communications specialist. In the not-too-distant past, it was a single account planner, or even an account director, in the agency looking at a single consumer in his or her whole-life context. Today there is an array of specialists, each with some strategic capability but each focused on their own space, with a one-dimensional view of the consumer and loyal to their own piece, which they guard ferociously.

That leaves the marketing management to decide what is needed, shop for the individual pieces and coordinate their efforts. It is not that marketers of today are skilled communications specialists while their forbears were not. It is that today's advertising and related agencies are narrowly focused and not performing the wider role that their forbears did. Someone has to do that job, and marketers are doing it themselves.

In recent years, some of the biggest global marketers have put their entire communications business up for competitive review, inviting not the individual advertising agencies and their direct marketing, PR and other cousins, but their parent holding companies—like WPP, IPG, and Publicis. This is in the obvious expectation that the holding companies will provide a single point of contact and pull together the best of resources across disciplines.

In 2016 WPP announced, with the usual fanfare, Global Team Blue (GTB), an expansion of their dedicated Ford unit, Blue Hive, 'on six continents across forty-nine offices…WPP's largest agency team with more than 2,000 members of staff'. In 2017 they announced over 100 layoffs. In 2018 Ford put their business up for review, threatening one of the world's oldest agency-client relationships: JWT first worked with Ford on the Model T, in 1910–12!

Even as GTB were being put on notice, WPP announced a collaboration with Unilever Foundry—Unilever's 'platform for start-ups and innovators to engage, collaborate and explore business ideas with Unilever and our 400+ brands'. In effect, via Foundry, Unilever—which once worked strictly within the framework of 'aligned' agencies—opened the doors to all comers. Not to be left out, WPP announced Team Unilever, cobbled together from a dozen WPP agencies, cohabiting Foundry's offices in Singapore.

Hard on the heels of that—announced on the same day, in fact—from another corner of WPP came another development: Ogilvy & Mather announced its 're-founding'. In a bold move, doing exactly the opposite of the lamentable fragmentation in the industry, the agency was doing away with all of its sub-brands—Ogilvy & Mather Advertising, Ogilvy One, Ogilvy Public Relations and others—and getting back to a single agency, a single brand, with a common client service model and P&L. This was a return to what those of a certain vintage have known as the full-service agency. To those who are familiar with its history and culture, Ogilvy was going back to David Ogilvy's 'One agency, indivisible'. In fact, it was doing away with Mather too, calling itself just Ogilvy.

WPP is not the only one pulling and pushing in different directions. The entire business is rife with such pressures as it feels its way around, as much as its clients do, for a way to deal with an increasingly complex and competitive business environment. What will work remains to be seen and will remain so for a long time. Chances are that once again the conductor's baton will pass to the marketer's hand.

'...40 years from now, those reticent parent companies, with their aggressively unexciting names, may well have earned their tentative new designation as the new full-service agencies,' wrote Jeremy Bullmore in 2004.[2]

Even as all this is happening, consulting firms are increasingly getting into the marketing services and communications space, acquiring all manner of specialist shops, and speculation is rife that the biggest agency holding companies—WPP and Publicis—are likely takeover targets for a firm like Accenture.

2 'Who's going to sit at the client's top table?' *Admap,* October 2004

Ironically, this is the time when communications strategists are more important than ever before. With rapid fragmentation of traditional mass media; new technologies offering ever-increasing media options; and changing social structures and behavioural modes, getting to the same person is becoming increasingly complex. Marketing is, in the end, about people and its purpose is to get them to do something. Pricing, logistics, distribution, etc., are only tools to facilitate and support behaviour. The *raison d'etre* of marketing is to build and to manage the consumer's relationship with that ephemeral something called a brand.

# CHAPTER 2
# What Is a Brand?

Amid the mergers and acquisitions mania of the 1980s, there was a seminal moment for marketing. This was when, in 1985, Philip Morris acquired General Foods and paid 3.2 times the book value of the company to do so. When asked the reason, Philip Morris executives told an astonished investor community that the assets they had paid for were not machinery and buildings, but brand names like Maxwell House, Kool-Aid, Jell-O and Tang.

Few could know better. Philip Morris was, after all, the owner of Marlboro—one of the world's best-known brands, an icon of masculinity around the world.

And so 'brand equity' acquired a real meaning. A company recognised brands as not merely trademarks but assets that could be leveraged for profit, and paid for them accordingly.

For all the talk about brands, company managements were until then—as many are to this day—focused on production as the primary activity of business. You made your products as efficiently as you could and if your product was better than your competitor's, you could charge more for it. Of course, you employed all relevant means to sell your product: gave it a distinctive name, priced it appropriately, distributed it, made it conveniently available and promoted it.

That single act on the part of Philip Morris stood the business paradigm on its head. The 'B-word' came out of marketing departments and advertising agencies, and into corporate boardrooms.

But the frenzy was short-lived—at least, the rush in that particular direction was. Eight years later, on 2 April 1993, Philip Morris once again made a bold move that created confusion in the ranks. On 'Marlboro Friday', as that day came to be known, the company announced a 20% reduction in the price of its flagship cigarette brand, Marlboro, to compete with generic no-name cigarettes (they literally came in plain white packages with no name on them) and bargain brands that were eating into its market.

The growth of generics and store brands had obviously meant the decline of premium brands. The market share of Marlboro, for instance, had fallen from as much as 30% to 22%. Manufacturers of premium brands, like Philip Morris, responded to falling volumes by pushing up prices to maintain profits. Manufacturers of generics, on the other hand, kept prices down to maintain volume, and the price gap kept widening.

Philip Morris, which just a few years earlier had paid good money to buy brand names, was going to compete at the commodities end of the market, that too with its flagship brand! What surer statement could there be that the day of the brand was over? 'The brand is dead!' went the cry. Stock prices of manufacturers of household brands dived: Coca-Cola, Procter & Gamble, Nabisco and, of course, Philip Morris. 'The Value Generation' was the new buzz phrase, to describe a consumer who could see through the puffery and tell true value.

The passage of time revealed that in dropping the price of Marlboro, Philip Morris was far from being defensive. On the contrary, it had seized the initiative. Consumers may well be willing to pay a premium for your brand, but the question is, how much? Philip Morris was not discounting Marlboro: it was correcting the price. The outcome was that cheap brands were destroyed; Marlboro regained its lost market share within two years and prices of both premium brands and generics rose. The stock price of Philip Morris not only recovered but also improved.

In a sense, 'Marlboro Friday' was only a dramatic reaffirmation of a phenomenon occurring around the world for some years. Easy availability of technology meant quality products could be manufactured much more widely and cheaply than they used to be. Thus, soap or breakfast cereal made by a small company and sold locally was often not noticeably inferior to that made by a multinational giant like Unilever or Kellogg but was cheaper, whether sold unbranded at the neighbourhood grocer's or as a store brand at a supermarket.

In fact, major corporations, competing to protect their volumes, became suppliers of the own-brand products of supermarket chains. The same frozen peas, for instance, would be packed and sold as the manufacturer's brand as well as supplied to the supermarket in its own name. 'The consumer is not a moron,' as David Ogilvy famously said. She could tell there was no difference between the two products and smartly bought the cheaper one. With parity products and parity pricing, the only differential was the brand.

What was happening in mass consumer markets was also taking place at the other end, in technology, albeit in a slightly different way.

With its launch of the 'Personal Computer' in 1981, IBM (not many know today that 'Personal Computer' was IBM's name for its desktop machine) had for the first time embraced open architecture, basing its new machine on an Intel chip and Microsoft's MS-DOS software. What this did was to open the floodgates for copycats with low priced clones, and IBM had to slash its prices to compete.

IBM was doing itself in, in other ways, too. As it grew in size and expanded the scope of its technology as well as its geographical spread, the company became highly decentralised. Each business was a fief, doing what it thought was best for itself. In a 180-degree turnaround from the old regimented days of its famous pinstripe suits and white shirts, IBM's marketing had become anarchic. People didn't talk to each other. They would go out to sell their products and denigrate other IBM products.

In 1993, hard on the heels of Marlboro Friday, came a surprising announcement from IBM: its new Chairman was Louis V Gerstner, then Chairman and CEO of RJR Nabisco. Prior to Nabisco he had worked for eleven years at American Express where he was Chairman and CEO of American Express Travel Related Services Company. Before that, he was with McKinsey, which he had joined in 1965. So he had no background in technology, other than the engineering degree he had acquired before his MBA from Harvard. What was he, a consumer marketing man, going to do with an ailing computer manufacturing giant?

Gerstner moved quickly to make many changes. The one that concerns us here, however, is that early in his tenure he consolidated IBM's advertising account, hitherto handled autonomously in different markets by more than forty advertising agencies, into one agency worldwide (Ogilvy & Mather, with which he had worked when at American Express), and launched a global advertising campaign for IBM.

Interesting, but how significant was that? The answer lies in Interbrand's annual ranking of the world's most valuable brands.[3] IBM, which came in at 282 in 1994, was number three in 1995. *Financial Times* reported: 'The IBM brand, valued at $17 billion, has skyrocketed since last year when it was labelled "worthless". IBM recaptures its *Financial World* ranking as the world's third most valuable brand, after coming in at 282 last

3 *The Best Global Brands* report, published annually by Interbrand Corporation, identifies the world's 100 most valuable brands. It was earlier done for the *Financial World* magazine and was called 'The World's Most Valuable Brands'.

year. The magazine attributes the rebound to "draconian cost cutting" and advertising that focuses on the IBM brand name.'

**Table 2.1: The World's Most Valuable Brands**

| **The world's most valuable brands** | | | |
|---|---|---|---|
| **1994 Rank** | **1995 Rank** | **Brand** | **1995 Value ($ bn)** |
| 1 | 1 | Coca-Cola | 39.0 |
| 2 | 2 | Marlboro | 38.7 |
| 282 | 3 | IBM | 17.1 |
| 8 | 4 | Motorola | 15.3 |
| 10 | 5 | Hewlett-Packard | 13.2 |

*Source*: Interbrand

IBM spent about $500 million on advertising that year and added $17 billion to the financial value of its brand: not a bad return on investment.

Note, too, that Marlboro—after the price cut that was widely seen to signal the death of brands—continued to be the world's second most valuable brand in the years that immediately followed that event.

There is perhaps no better illustration of brand value than the two great colas, because there is perhaps no better example of two brands famously fighting head to head with parity products, parity pricing and parity distribution. Yet there are those who will choose one over the other every time. This is not because the other is less convenient to use, or will not quench their thirst, or costs more, or is not as easily available, but because they feel differently about the two.

That difference is enough to have made Coca-Cola the world's most valuable brand. Interbrand placed it consistently at number one in the world up to 2012, after which it was overtaken by Apple and Google. In the 2018 rankings Coca-Cola came in at number five after Apple, Google, Amazon and Microsoft, but was still by far the top packaged goods brand—in fact, the top non-technology brand—while Pepsi, which has never been in the top ten, came in at number twenty-two.

**Table 2.2: The World's Most Valuable Brands, 2018**

| The world's most valuable brands, 2018 | | |
|---|---|---|
| **Rank** | **Brand** | **Value ($ bn)** |
| 1 | Apple | 214.5 |
| 2 | Google | 155.5 |
| 3 | Amazon | 100.8 |
| 4 | Microsoft | 92.7 |
| 5 | Coca-Cola | 66.3 |
| 6 | Samsung | 59.9 |
| 7 | Toyota | 53.4 |
| 8 | Mercedes-Benz | 48.6 |
| 9 | Facebook | 45.2 |
| 10 | McDonald's | 43.4 |
| 22 | Pepsi | 20.8 |

*Source*: Interbrand

Closer home, when The Coca-Cola Company re-entered India in the early 1990s, it acquired Thums Up from Parle for a reported price of ₹1,800 million. Launched in 1977, in the void left by the exit of Coca-Cola from the country, Thums Up was the leading carbonated soft drink in India. What Coca-Cola bought was not plant and machinery or a fleet of trucks, or even stocks of glass bottles: those belonged to the bottlers. All it bought was the intellectual property, the exclusive right to use the Thums Up name and symbol.

In giving a financial interpretation to the concept of brands, Interbrand typically examines three key aspects that contribute to a brand's valuation:

1. *The financial performance of the branded products or service*: That must be the primary concern. All said and done, that is why a company owns a brand.
2. *The role the brand plays in influencing consumer choice*: In the words of Norman Berry, former Creative Director at Ogilvy & Mather: 'A brand must, in the eyes of the consumer—and thus the retailer—have *no adequate direct substitute.*' That is what a brand really means. A Pepsi may fulfil the need if you can't get a Coke (or, in fairness, the other way round), but it doesn't quite satisfy in the same way; it is not an *adequate direct substitute.*
3. *The strength the brand has to command a premium price, or secure earnings for the company*: If a brand has no adequate direct substitute, it must be able to command a premium price or deliver stable and secure earnings. Otherwise, what's the difference between it and an unbranded commodity?

So what is a brand? Theodore Levitt called it 'a complex cluster of value satisfactions', and went on to say, 'The generic thing is not itself the product; it is merely, as in poker, table stakes—the minimum that is necessary at the outset to give its producer a chance to play the game.'[4]

Jeremy Bullmore, long-time Chairman of J Walter Thompson, London, and one of the finest writers in and about advertising, put it like this:

4 Theodore Levitt, 'Marketing Success through Differentiation—of Anything', *Harvard Business Review* (Jan–Feb 1980), https://hbr.org/1980/01/marketing-success-through-differentiation-of-anything. Oddly, Levitt used the term 'the generic thing' instead of product and 'product' when he meant what we call a brand.

> ...people build brands...as birds build nests—from scraps and straws we chance upon. We imbue everything about that brand, however trivial, with meaning and significance.... People build brands in their heads—whether or not the owners of the brand intend them to.[5]

In those few words Bullmore said a mouthful. First, that it is consumers who build brands; marketers (the brand's owners) only supply the raw material, be it advertisements or packaging or news. Where else would consumers build them, but in their own heads and hearts? That is where brands exist—not in factories, not in shops. Second, consumers do not go looking for material, but build them with the 'scraps and straws' they happen to come across. Third—and this should be of concern to marketers—they use what they will, whether you intend them to or not. That includes not only the good things, such as a magazine picture of a celebrity wearing your brand, but also the bad things: what they heard from someone about your poor service; their struggle to claim compensation after an accident with your delivery truck; or a news item about the exploitation of labour.

If that seems fatalistic—that whatever you do, people will reach the conclusions they will—take heart from the words of Sir Michael Perry, former Chairman of Unilever:

> [A brand is] nothing more or less than the sum of all the mental connections people have around [the product]. Memories from childhood, something your mum said...and in the case of newer brands memories from ads. *The trick is to arrange things so that the mental connections are enhancing.*[6]

5 Jeremy Bullmore, *Behind the Scenes in Advertising*, 2nd ed. (Oxfordshire: NTC Publications, 1998).

6 Sir Michael Perry's speech at the European Marketing Conference in 1996.

Much of the discussion about marketing communications centres on advertising. This is clearly because advertising is the most visible and most expensive element of the communications mix, and is often the first and most frequent interaction between the consumer and the brand.

Often advertising sets up expectations from the brand with the introductory greeting, the first handshake. What the consumer experiences of the product, at retail and other points of interaction, must be in keeping with those expectations.

Putting it all together and making the elements work consistently and synergistically is what we call integrated marketing communications. And when we arrange things well we make the mental connections enhancing.

**'You can be watching TV and see Coca-Cola, and you can know that the President drinks Coke, Liz Taylor drinks Coke, and just think, you can drink Coke too. A Coke is a Coke, and no amount of money can get you a better Coke than the one the bum on the corner is drinking. All Cokes are the same and all Cokes are good. Liz Taylor knows it, the President knows it, the bum knows it and you know it.'**

***—Andy Warhol***

*The Philosophy of Andy Warhol*

***

**'In a world full of right and wrong, good and bad, meaningful and trivial, advertising is the one force that respects the individual for what she is. It speaks to what we want to be and not what we should be. It associates us with images we crave to belong to, without casting judgment on whether we deserve to.'**

***—Santosh Desai***

# CHAPTER 3
# Making the Mental Connections Enhancing

Whether you are selling fertiliser to farmers or coffee to young urban adults or treatment for diarrhoea to mothers of babies or airline seats to international travellers, there are three fundamental truths. First, no one actually needs another brand. Second, people do not look for marketing messages. Third, everything communicates.

As people go through their daily lives—read newspapers and magazines, watch television, post messages on social media, travel, shop, see and meet other people—marketing messages intrude into their lives. No one turns on the television or opens a newspaper to look at the ads; no one opens an email hoping for a promotion offer; no one goes to a mall to look at in-shop displays and collect leaflets. Intruding, however, is not necessarily the same as being unwelcome. Communication that provides useful information, helps solve a problem, empathises, reassures, or simply amuses, entertains and creates good feelings, can be welcome, even if unsolicited.

From everything they see and experience, people form impressions based on fact or on feeling. When they put their money down to buy something, they do so in response to all that they processed inside their heads. That is how brands are created, and they exist nowhere but in the heads and hearts of people.

What really is marketing, though? Many definitions have been written, most notably by pundits like Philip Kotler. Most of them centre on the two thoughts of exchange and profit. This means that marketing essentially involves providing goods or services in exchange for money, with one of the parties (presumably the one supplying the goods or services) making a profit in the process. In August 2004, the American Marketing Association unveiled its new definition of marketing:

> Marketing is an organisational function and a set of processes for creating, communicating and delivering value to customers and for managing customer relationships in ways that benefit the organisation and its stakeholders.[7]

All such definitions are limiting, however. The AMA definition is inward looking and organisation-centric and even Kotler's classic 'satisfying needs and wants through an exchange process'[8] is inadequate to explain his own 'generic concept of marketing'.[9]

Marketing is also described, if not defined, in terms of the 4Ps: Product, Price, Place (i.e., distribution) and Promotion.[10] However, the 4Ps are simply the elements, the activities of marketing. To have a product (or a service), obviously at a price, and make it available (distribution, or place) merely means you have something to promote. But the marketing loop is closed only when your prospective

7 The first official definition of marketing was adopted in 1935 by the National Association of Marketing Teachers, a predecessor of the American Marketing Association (AMA). It was reviewed and reaffirmed by the AMA in 1948 and again in 1960, and revised only in 1985.

8 First expounded in Kotler's classic text, *Marketing Management: Analysis, Planning, Implementation and Control.*

9 See Chapter 8, 'Your Company Is Also a Brand'.

10 Again Kotler's concept, which he later updated to the 4Cs: Convenience, Communication, Cost to the user and Customer needs. Jagdish Sheth has posited another framework, the four As: Acceptability, Affordability, Accessibility and Awareness.

customers do what you want them to do, which is usually to buy the product and in most cases not just once but repeatedly.

Thus, marketing is about people, and the whole point of marketing is to *get them to do what you want them to do*—buy your product, not just once but repeatedly, pay their taxes, breastfeed their babies, etc. In social marketing, it is often to *get them to not do what you don't want them to do*—not give dowry, not drink and drive and so on. The elements of the marketing mix, the 4Ps, are merely the buttons you press, or the levers you pull, to get people to voluntarily do what you want them to.

Marketing is not an act, but a process. What specifically you do is not important; that your prospects do what you intend them to, is. This, then, is my definition of marketing:

> Marketing is the process of inducing a mass of people to exercise their choices and behave consistently over time in a manner desired by the marketer.

Note especially the words 'induce' and 'behave'. Behaviour is the outcome you seek and you can only create the right conditions for it: you cannot demand or legislate it. What you do to induce that behaviour depends on the marketing context and, in all but the most mature categories, must necessarily extend way beyond advertising.

People don't consciously distinguish between what they see and hear in a television commercial and what they read in a newspaper article or in a tweet or a Facebook post: they simply take it in and keep it, actively reject it or passively forget it. Thus, if the celebrity who endorses your brand is in the news for a scandal, your customers do not distinguish the ad from the news: they associate the event with your brand, though you would rather they did not. You meant them to associate your brand with the celebrity, and the more successful you have been, the stronger will be the connection and the resultant reaction. That is why Pepsi terminated its contract with Michael Jackson and ended its very successful advertising campaign as soon as he was accused of child molestation, without waiting to know whether he was guilty.

The more you direct and control the supply of 'raw material' so that it is consistent with your purpose, the more you can 'make the mental connections enhancing', the more surely you influence the opinions and feelings created about your brand. For in the end, as brands exist only in the heads and hearts of consumers, it is what people think and feel about it that defines a brand.

A most articulate—even if unintended—endorsement comes from an unlikely quarter. Naomi Klein in her anti-brand manifesto says, '...the brands that exited the downturn running were the ones who opted for marketing over value every time: Nike, Apple, the Body Shop, Calvin Klein, Disney, Levi's and Starbucks...They integrated the idea of branding into the very fabric of their companies...These companies didn't wear their image like a cheap shirt—their image was so integrated with their business that other people wore it as their shirt.'[11]

Geoffrey Randall in his slim book, *Branding,*[12] gives the whole idea a simple construct:

1. Every brand must have some means of communicating with its buyers. This may not be advertising, but it must be direct if it is to be controllable.
2. Many other methods of communication...can be used to...multiply the effects of advertising.

---

11 Naomi Klein, *No Logo* (London: Harper Collins Publishers, 2001), 20–34. Read it for an articulate thesis on brands and marketing communications.

12 Geoffrey Randall, *Branding: A Practical Guide to Planning Your Strategy* (London: Kogan Page, 1997).

3. All the means of communication and the messages transmitted must be coordinated to make sure that they are saying the same thing.

Often several means of communication are employed, but the problem is that their employment is piecemeal, and they do not work in synergy. If they did, they could enhance the value of the whole: in fact, they are frequently unrelated, if not actually in contradiction.

Integrating your brand's marketing communications involves understanding several roles and relationships:

1. *Defining your target in terms of your category and brand*: Are you targeting current users, new users or lapsed users? If current users, is it to retain their loyalty or to increase consumption or to upgrade them to a premium product? If new users, what do they do now? Why should they change? Why did lapsed users lapse? What will bring them back?
2. *Buyers, users and influencers*: Who plays what role? Is the buyer a user, an enabler or a gatekeeper? Does anyone have a veto? Whose opinion matters in the purchase process? In use situations?
3. *Contact points*: What media are they exposed to: passive or active? When and in what situations are they most receptive *to the kind of message we have to communicate*?
4. *What do you have to do to people to get the desired result*: Help them be better informed? Force a comparison? Move them emotionally? Assuage their fears and worries?
5. *Communication channels*: What do different channels do best? Like a set of tools in a toolbox, different channels—advertising, public relations, direct marketing, events, etc.—have different strengths. You can always use the back end of a screwdriver to hammer a nail, but that is not the best tool for the job. On the other hand, if the only tool you have is a hammer, you will see every problem as a nail.

> You need access to the whole toolbox, to understand what each tool is good for, and to know which tools are best for the task at hand. But you don't have to use all the tools in the toolbox: *only the ones needed to do the job best.*

Integration can be at different levels:

*Brand consistency*: At the simplest level, integrated marketing communications means keeping everything you say about or do with the brand consistent with the brand's audience, proposition and values, so that no conflicting messages are sent out. If that seems self-evident, just a hygiene factor, it is: and that is why it is surprising how often it is violated or simply overlooked in the interest of expediency. Or perhaps because, in the words of Wally Olins, 'the brand manager—frequently a young marketing person on the way up the commercial ladder—sometimes uses temporary occupation of the brand to demonstrate flair and originality at the expense of brand consistency'.[13]

*Bringing advertising to life*: That done, a smart marketer with strong advertising will try to bring the brand's advertising to life, to acquire a meaning (and so help the brand acquire a meaning) outside of the television commercial and beyond the product category, in the context of the consumer's life. Not all advertising is big enough in its meaning to enable that and this makes such opportunities all the more valuable. To not do so, when your brand and your advertising afford you the opportunity, is to waste an asset.

*Using multiple contact points for the same audience*: The bigger the change you seek in perception and behaviour, the more likely you are to have to use several contact points. New ideas, new ways of doing things involve some kind of risk—not simply financial, as in the price of the product, but often performance risk (Will it do what it is supposed to? Will I be able to use/ do it properly?), social risk (What will people think of me for using/ doing this?)

13 Wally Olins, *Corporate Identity* (Boston: Harvard Business School Press, 1990).

or self-image risk (What kind of person does that make me?). Consumers can start out with interest, but drop out because they do not have answers to these questions. It is for the marketer to close the loop and complete the process by providing them not only the relevant information but often also the reassurance that they are doing the right thing.

No single channel or means of communication is enough for that. Often multiple channels are used—indeed, this is the most commonly understood meaning of integrated marketing communications—but simply using multiple channels is not integration. They have to work in conjunction to induce the target audience to think, feel and do as you intend them to. Too often the elements of the brand's marketing plan are not in synergy or strategic fit, because they are not planned in that fashion. Tactical responses to situations are of course a reality of business, but there is really no reason why such responses cannot be within a determined strategic framework.

*Addressing multiple audiences*: As we have seen, purchase decisions are often made jointly by two or more persons with differing needs from the category and the brand. Equally, there may be one decision maker, but one or more influencers. The influence they exert may be in the capacity of actual users (children, for toys), facilitators (banks, for financed purchases), or experts (doctors, for healthcare products). It is then essential for the marketer to address all the links in the value chain, *each in the terms relevant to their role in the purchase decision.* That necessitates an understanding of their roles as well as which channel works best with whom to achieve what outcome.

In the chapters that follow, we will recount examples of successful integrated marketing communications programmes, and outline an approach to developing them.

**Do This or Die**

**Is this ad some kind of trick?**

**No. But it could have been.**

**And at exactly that point rests a do or die decision for American business.**

**We in advertising, together with our clients, have all the power and skill to trick people.**

**Or so we think. But we're wrong.**

**We can't fool any of the people any of the time.**

**There is indeed a twelve-year-old mentality in this country; every six-year-old has one.**

**We are a nation of smart people.**

**And most smart people ignore most advertising because most advertising ignores smart people.**

**Instead we talk to each other.**

**We debate endlessly about the medium and the message.**

**Nonsense. In advertising, the message itself is the message.**

**A blank page and a blank television screen are one and the same.**

**And above all, the messages we put on those pages and on those television screens must be the truth.**

**For if we play tricks with the truth, we die.**

**Now. The other side of the coin.**

**Telling the truth about a product demands a product that's worth telling the truth about.**

**Sadly, so many products aren't.**

**So many products don't do anything better.**

**Or anything different.**

**So many don't work quite right.**

**Or don't last. Or simply don't matter.**

**If we also play this trick, we also die.**

**Because advertising only helps a bad product fail faster.**

**No donkey chases the carrot forever.**

**He catches on. And quits.**

**That's the lesson to remember.**

**Unless we do, we die.**

**Unless we change, the tidal wave of consumer indifference will wallop into the mountain of advertising and manufacturing drivel.**

**That day we die.**

**We'll die in our marketplace.**

**On our shelves. In our gleaming packages of empty promises.**

**Not with a bang. Not with a whimper.**

**But by our own skilled hands.**

***—Doyle Dane Bernbach***

*House Advertisement of Advertising Agency, late 1960s*

# CHAPTER 4
# Cadbury's Cocoa Cultivation Programme

In early 1986, Adi Lakshmanan, Vice President of Marketing at Cadbury India[14], called in his advertising agency, Ogilvy & Mather, with an unusual brief: to develop a campaign targeted at farmers, urging them to plant more cocoa.

Cadbury began marketing chocolates in India in 1948, and were for many years the only significant marketer of chocolates in the country. In 1973 came Amul, marketed by the Gujarat Cooperative Milk Marketing Federation, which was already the leading brand of dairy products, but Cadbury continued to dominate the chocolate market. Now the company was anticipating the entry of Nestlé[15] and, with the corresponding growth in the market, the demand for cocoa to outstrip supply in the future. Unless steps were immediately taken to increase the production of cocoa, there would be a shortage five years hence.

Instead of preparing to corner the raw material that was its own lifeblood and starve the competition, Cadbury chose to catalyse an increase in supply. Recognising that the supply depended on a large number of individuals, they took the approach of marketing to them, to induce them to act voluntarily in their own enlightened self-interest. This was truly the response of a leader.

---

14 The company was then Hindustan Cocoa Products, but was popularly referred to as Cadbury. The name was later changed to Cadbury India, and is now Mondelez India. Its house brand used to be Cadbury's and, now is Cadbury.

15 Nestlé launched chocolates in India in 1991.

## Understanding the Issues

In 1965, Cadbury India began to promote and support commercial cultivation of cocoa. Until then a small supply was imported to meet the needs of a small market. Between 1968 and 1973 the company imported 7,000 kg of cocoa seeds from Malaysia, and distributed over five million seedlings free of cost to farmers in the potential cocoa-growing state of Kerala and the contiguous districts of Karnataka and Tamil Nadu.

In 1974, the first commercial output of fifty tonnes was achieved, which grew to 1,000 tonnes by 1980. On account of an unplanned halt in their own production in 1980, Cadbury were unable to buy and use that year's crop. As they were the only buyer of cocoa in the country, there was no alternative use for the produce. Almost the entire output was wasted, and growers suffered losses. Farmers who had ventured into the crop pulled it out and went back to their conventional crops.

In 1986, when they were looking into future demand, Cadbury anticipated their own need in 1990 at 5,000 tonnes and the total market at 8,000 tonnes. As government policy precluded imports, this meant doubling the production in five years, from an estimated 4,000 tonnes in 1985: a growth unlikely to occur by itself, given the negligible increase in acreage between 1980 and 1985.[16]

The agricultural sector in India is made up of a very large number of small farmers with very small land holdings. In Kerala about 97% of agricultural land holdings are below one hectare.[17]

Thus a vast majority of farmers live from harvest to harvest, and have little or no capacity to invest or otherwise take risks with their crops. They also do not have enough land to experiment, by trying out a new crop or a new practice on one small part of the

---

16 The market is now about 30,000 tonnes a year, of which about 17,000 tonnes are domestically grown across Andhra Pradesh, Kerala, Tamil Nadu and Karnataka, while the rest is imported.

17 *Provisional Report on 9th Agricultural Census* (Thiruvananthapuram: Department of Economics and Statistics, Government of Kerala, 2013). Over 80% of these are, in fact, below half a hectare. Unlike most of India, in Kerala small and marginal farmers do grow cash crops, mostly coconut and areca nut.

farm, while continuing with their current practice on most of it. Thus, a farmer who adopts a new crop or a new practice literally bets the farm on it.

Cocoa, however, is a different story. It is a shade tree that grows in the aisles between rows of coconut or areca nut palms. In a grove of tall palms, where 40–50% sunlight penetration is possible, cocoa absorbs such solar energy as filters through, and its presence helps to make the soil conditions more beneficial for the main crop under which it takes shelter. Thus it maintains a symbiotic relationship with the main crop and, by growing in an otherwise unproductive space, generates additional income for the farmer.

When we, at Ogilvy & Mather, considered the task at hand, it was clear that the main proposition was the easy part. Cocoa represents a source of additional income for coconut and areca nut farmers, with no risk to their main crop: it is, if anything, beneficial. That idea was not hard to sell. But why, if planting cocoa was such an attractive proposition on the face of it, were more farmers not planting it?

Living in Bombay, we were far removed from farmers in Kerala, from their hopes and ambitions, problems and concerns. So we sent a cross-discipline team to travel through Kerala, meeting and talking to farmers, Cadbury's own team of cocoa advisors, and others associated with the subject. Their brief was to understand, first hand and in depth, what was happening on the ground, so that we could address the barriers that stood between the farmer and cocoa.

We uncovered a complex network of roles and influences, problems and concerns. The good news was that the proposition was wholly credible: the fact that cocoa grows in an otherwise unproductive space was known and understood, as was the simple idea that it represented an opportunity to earn more from the same land.

What came home to us strongly, though, was the strength of feeling generated by the mishap of 1980. While their main crop was unaffected by it, a large number of small and marginal farmers had lost the money and effort they had spent on the cocoa crop. Those affected were bitter about it, and those who had not planted cocoa before had learnt from the experience of their neighbours.

Our first task was to revive their interest in the proposition. There was no better way than showing them the success stories of their fellow farmers. Thankfully, Kerala is a state with a very high level of literacy and of newspaper readership. It is, in fact, the only state in India in which you could not only reach small farmers by advertising in the newspapers, but even afford to use long copy to convey information! We found several farmers who were willing to be quoted and recorded their testimonials. These formed the basis for a series of newspaper advertisements setting out the proposition—that there was extra money to be earned from the same land—and the experiences of farmers who had benefited from it.

Every crop is unique, and a farmer wanting to plant cocoa would need to know a lot about it: everything from the right soil conditions to the right cultivation practices. It was important that he gets the right information and advice, so he could start off correctly; indeed that he start with good quality seeds too. Cadbury already had a team of specialist cocoa advisers in Kerala and an experimental farm at Chundale, in Wynad district, headed by an experienced planter.

We gave the existing support system a name and a logo. All communication on the programme was put out and signed off by Cadbury's Cocoa Advisory Service. Every advertisement included a coupon to aid response, and farmers who wrote in (thousands did) got a detailed information pack and the offer of either free seeds or seedlings at a subsidised price of 30 paise each. The team of cocoa advisors fanned out all over Kerala, meeting farmers, following up on the mailing and encouraging them to take the next step.

The advertisements ran in the leading daily newspapers of the state, *Malayala Manorama* and *Mathrubhumi*. Print was supported by hoardings, wall paintings, banners, radio spots and a film screened in over 230 cinemas in 189 towns.

Against the backdrop of 1980, though, that was not enough. After all, this was Cadbury telling farmers to plant cocoa—the same Cadbury that had initiated them into cocoa earlier and a few years ago had not bought their produce. How could they have confidence this time around?

In fact, 1986 was a very different time. The government of Rajiv Gandhi was still new, the first wave of liberalisation had begun and India was suffused with a new-found optimism. The world was looking to India to do business, the future looked good, and so did the outlook for Cadbury as well as for cocoa. In fact, it was the anticipated growth in demand for the crop that had prompted Cadbury to take this initiative in the first place. In the overall bullish environment that was India, it was necessary to create a positive, supportive backdrop of knowledge against which prospective cocoa growers would receive this communication.

Though Cadbury were sparking the interest of farmers, neither was it feasible for them to single-handedly support the cultivation of cocoa in the country nor was it their role to do so. It was necessary to generate action from the appropriate government agencies, whose task it was to support farmers. For that, we had to create interest among decision makers and influencers in the central and state governments and related bodies, to whom cocoa was until then a minor crop, and get them to see its potential. Only then would they be induced to mobilise resources to complement the company's own field extension services to support cocoa.

We mounted what would usually be called a public relations programme, but in this case, is perhaps more appropriately called a public information programme. We approached the two leading Kerala newspapers as well as Doordarshan and All India Radio (AIR)[18] and got them interested in the subject. Importantly, we did not hide the facts or try to obfuscate the public memory of 1980. On the contrary, we showed them the difference in the times and, therefore, in the prospects. Consequently, they became willing allies in spreading the good word about the prospects for cocoa in the context of the economic climate in the country in general and the increasing consumption of chocolate in particular. They carried stories and interviews about cocoa, Cadbury, the chocolate business in India and internationally, and of course the general economic context. All of this created a buzz about cocoa, a positive environment in which the farmer saw our advertisements.

AIR had a daily farm programme to bring farmers information and advice on cultivation practices. It was a programme all farmers were aware of and found helpful, and tuned in to as a matter of practice. However, it covered coconut, areca nut and paddy, but ignored cocoa. We knew it would be a vital means of dissemination of information if we could leverage it. We spoke to the officials at AIR and found that their priorities were determined (quite rightly) by the state's Department of Agriculture. So we had meetings with the department, armed with the recent articles and reports in the press as well as other published data, and persuaded them that as a large number of farmers were taking to cocoa cultivation, it was in their interest to include cocoa in the farm programme of AIR. We succeeded: the department gave the necessary instructions, Cadbury provided technical information support, and AIR ran programmes giving advice on cocoa cultivation.

So there we were: a positive buzz in the environment, advertising to place the specific proposition before the farmer; and technical support provided by Cadbury and the relevant

18 This was before the advent of cable and satellite television. Government-owned Doordarshan (TV) and AIR were the only broadcasting networks in the country.

government agencies, including AIR. A seemingly small but critical element in the print advertising was the coupon, to enable prospects to 'raise their hands'. This is an important device to help you identify, out of the general population who receive your communication, those who are inclined to act now—the best and most likely prospects. Respondents were sent detailed information, and offered subsidised seedlings and personalised expert advice.

When you set out to run a mass communication programme, you do not know one individual from another. But the fact is that they are not all the same, and even among those who are interested, some are likely to act sooner than others. They may appear alike in terms of demographics, but two neighbours or two brothers will respond differently, depending on their mental make-up, needs and desires, propensity to take risks, past experience and resources. You must be able to either identify your best prospects, the ones with the greater inclination to act, or provide them the facility to be able to contact you and identify themselves. Then you can provide information, guidance, assurance or whatever they need to be able to take the next steps. That is the role of coupons and contact numbers in advertisements and of direct contact programmes, which enable face-to-face communication.

To increase the scope and scale of direct contact with farmers, we mounted a van operation. Manned by a staff of four, including a trained presenter, and equipped with audio-visual equipment, the van travelled through Kerala, visiting a different village *shandy* or *haat*[19] each day. It covered about forty-five of them across eight districts over a two-month journey cycle.

At each stop the van was met by one of Cadbury's cocoa advisors, and went through a set routine. Playing our cocoa theme

19 Rural India has a system of 'market days'. On a designated day, a cluster of villages has a *shandy* or *haat* at which farmers and traders from surrounding areas gather to do business, buying and selling not only livestock, poultry and farm inputs, but also consumer goods. The markets operate to a fixed calendar. Some are weekly, others less frequent; some are specialised, dealing in only livestock, for example, while others are of a more general nature.

song to attract attention, the presenter gathered a crowd and told the farmers of the benefits of cocoa cultivation. The cocoa advisor answered their questions, and distributed a leaflet giving detailed information and a contact address. Predictably, those more interested stayed behind and spoke to the cocoa advisor in detail. This routine was repeated several times in a typical three-hour market stop. In the afternoon the van would visit surrounding villages and repeat the routine, to reach those who may not have visited the market that day.

At night, as the van and the equipment were doing nothing in particular, we set up a screen in an open field and ran a popular feature film that was free for all, interspersed with the 'commercial' we were running in the cinemas.

## Marketing to Current 'Customers'

All this was to bring more farmers and more acreage into cocoa, but the output would take time: the cocoa plant starts yielding fruit in the third year after planting; starts giving economic returns in the fifth; and reaches full production after the eighth. In the short term, therefore, we had to increase the realisation of beans from current growers. A small farmer not only produces a small quantity of beans but also has limited means. If he had to travel a long distance or otherwise go through a great deal of trouble to get the beans to the buyer, either he would get fed up and give up, or he would lose time and the beans would be rendered useless, or both.

In more usual marketing terms, when the company is selling rather than buying, this is the difference between long-term growth and current volume, between getting new customers and increasing the consumption of current customers. When you set out to grow the market and get new users, you also need to ask whether your current users have the potential to consume more, and leverage their potential to do so. Frequently, the two need different programmes.

We took two kinds of steps. The first was to improve the efficiency of the 'distribution' network, which in this case was the collection network. We flagged Cadbury's collection centres by putting up direction signs and signboards; distributed a printed address list; and periodically ran a small print advertisement listing the addresses. We also increased the reach of the network by appointing collection agents to visit farmers, collect the beans and pay them at their doorstep. The second step we took was to help increase the output of the current farms by supporting government programmes for improving farm management and pest control practices.

The campaign ran for two years, or two planting seasons. As far as its outcome is concerned, whatever the resultant growth in acreage and in the tonnage produced, there was no shortage of cocoa despite the increase in demand, and by that measure it was successful. More relevant to our current purpose, the programme recognised that to get the farmer to plant cocoa it had to involve several constituents, and it did so in a manner that induced them to act in concert to achieve the desired result.

Broken down to its component parts, all the programme did was essentially this:

1. Make the proposition to the prospect (cocoa as a means of extra profit without extra investment).
2. Create a positive climate for communication to be received.
3. Get the best prospects to raise their hands.
4. Direct them to a source of information and nudge them into action.

The whole programme was really a marketing role reversal. In this case, the company was the buyer: it was marketing to potential sellers the idea of producing what it needed and facilitating them in selling to it. However, as long as it flows from the one to the many, the principles of marketing and of marketing communications remain the same.

# CHAPTER 5
# ORS Programme

Diarrhoea is the second biggest killer of infants and small children in India, next only to acute respiratory infection. Sadly, it need not be: the correct treatment for diarrhoea is inexpensive, easily available and easy to administer, but not enough is known about it. This is so not just among the poor and the uneducated, but in middle-class homes too.

Part of the problem is that in India, across regions and socio-economic levels, there are home remedies for almost everything, especially for simple ailments, and people rely on them all the more for infants. In the case of diarrhoea, the typical home remedy is a salt-sugar solution in water.

Diarrhoea seems simple enough, not something to rush to the doctor for, and indeed it is. What kills is not the diarrhoeal infection itself but the dehydration it causes. It is especially dangerous for infants and small children as their water loss-to-body mass ratio is much higher than in adults, which makes dehydration much riskier for them.

The condition is self-limiting. All that is needed is for it to be allowed to take its course while the body is rehydrated. Salt, sugar and water are all important but are not enough, and also must be taken in sufficient quantity and in the right proportions. The simple, universally available answer is packaged oral rehydration salts (ORS).[20] So huge is the problem of diarrhoea deaths in developing countries that the discovery of the science behind oral rehydration therapy was described by The Lancet as 'potentially the most important medical advance this century'.

ICICI Bank undertook to bring its management resources to bear on the problem under the aegis of its Programme for Advancement of Commercial Technology—Child and Reproductive Health (PACT-CRH), in which it worked with Indian industry to develop and promote sustainable products and services to help meet India's health goals. A two-year programme for the promotion of ORS in infant and child diarrhoea was funded by USAID and technical support was provided by Commercial Market Strategies (CMS). The communications programme was designed and led by McCann Healthcare along with McCann-Erickson (advertising), Result McCann (direct contact), Universal McCann (media) and Corporate Voice Weber Shandwick (public relations).

According to the National Family Health Survey 1998–99, the awareness of ORS was 62% nationally, but the usage was only 27%. The use of ORS was even lower in North India at 20% and the rates of child mortality were higher.

The campaign was focused on the urban areas of Uttar Pradesh, Uttarakhand, Madhya Pradesh, Chhattisgarh, Bihar, Jharkhand, Rajasthan and Delhi. The incidence of infant mortality and the use of ORS were equally poor in urban and rural areas. The urban areas were logistically easier to administer, for testing what looked like it was going to be a large, complex exercise.

## The Objective

What the communications programme sought to achieve was clear and single-minded: that ORS should be the first response in diarrhoea in infants and small children.

20 For a description of how ORS works, visit www.rehydrate.org.

Getting there, though, was not so simple. We were dealing with existing, entrenched practices that not only concerned health, but concerned the health of infants and small children. That was a subject on which every region and every community in India has its own traditional beliefs and home remedies. That also meant the young mother was subject to a host of influences and opinions from older women, and that the doctor was consulted only in acute conditions or emergencies.

The communication had to tread carefully. While positioning ORS as the first response in diarrhoea, it could neither describe ORS as a treatment nor denigrate antidiarrhoeal and antibiotic drugs, both of which clearly have their own relevance and utility.

## Understanding the Context

The proper prescription and treatment of a medical condition typically involves three constituents: the patient or care giver (in this case a young mother), a doctor, and a chemist. In the case of ORS, each of the three had a role to play in its low usage.

### *The mother*

At the beginning of the programme, awareness of ORS among target mothers (mothers of children below the age of five in the target markets) was 52%, but the extent of use was 20%.

Low awareness is easier to deal with: all you have to do is make them aware. How you deal with those who are aware but are not using it is more complex, and depends on your understanding of the barriers to usage. In the case of ORS it was not the price, the availability or the complexity in use. So what was it?

The occurrence of diarrhoea is not unusual, and the immediate need is to stop it. The mother does not see it as a serious condition; her concern is about the resultant weakness, and there are accepted, familiar home remedies to deal with it. Apart from salt-sugar solution, some of the other popular ones are *kanji* and coconut water. ORS is seen as nothing more than a packaged mixture of salt and sugar. She has both at home, so why would she need that packet?

Through this process, any older female relative—mother, mother-in-law, sister—and her husband participate, but they have the same beliefs and the same level of knowledge.

A lot of the time the condition plays itself out; often, sadly, it doesn't. When it does, normalcy is restored and the remedy is taken to have worked. When it doesn't, the mother feels a loss of control and, in the best instance, seeks medical help in panic. At that stage the doctor takes over and she does as advised.

### The doctor

A general practitioner or a paediatrician, the doctor typically prescribes antibiotics or antidiarrhoeal drugs.

As is well known in medical marketing, doctors don't usually prescribe lay treatments or even over-the-counter (OTC) drugs. What a doctor prescribes is a reflection of expertise. Indeed, patients are often disappointed if all they get is something that they might have done themselves. They feel their complaint has not been taken seriously, and that the doctor's fee was a waste of money. As we have all experienced, prescriptions often include one or two feel-good medicines or at least some instruction to be followed.

It was relatively rare for a doctor to prescribe ORS as the primary response in diarrhoea. If at all in the prescription, it would be an additional item; or it could be a suggestion made in passing; or even just an assenting nod in response to a mother's specific query. Indeed, studies showed that the actual incidence of prescription of ORS was far lower than was claimed by doctors.

Since the administration of ORS does not require any expertise and in fact should be immediate at home, we had to reach out to mothers. But, as everyone in medical marketing knows, doctors resent direct-to-patient communication unless their expertise is respected and they too are taken into confidence.

It was, therefore, important to reach out to doctors, so that even if they did not actively prescribe ORS, they at least did not dismiss it and hopefully, in the best instance, endorsed it.

The doctors to be contacted were not only paediatricians and general physicians but, very importantly, practitioners of Indian systems of medicine (known in the trade as ISMPs). Variously qualified, they practice a range of systems of medicine—homeopathy, Ayurveda, *siddha*, *yunani*, and others. Many of them have no formal qualifications—only experience and the faith of their patients. They were important because they usually serve the most vulnerable sections of the population. Medical marketers don't typically bother with them, so they are not jaded and desensitised by a barrage of marketing communications and are likely to be more receptive.

## *The chemist*

The chemist in India is not only a seller of medicines; he is often the prescriber for simple, everyday ailments like a headache, a cold or an upset stomach. This has much to do with not only the levels of education, but also the typical retail format, in which everything is behind the counter and the customer cannot pick up products, in this case OTC medicines, study the labels and decide what to buy.

The relevance of chemists to the ORS programme was at three levels. First, to stock ORS; second, to use their outlets as points of consumer contact; and, third, that if asked they should recommend ORS instead of antidiarrhoeal or antibiotic drugs for children.

## All ORS is Not Equal

So far we have been dealing with ORS as a generic product, and that is what the programme was meant to promote. But that is not what the customer finds in the shop, because several manufacturers make the product and it is sold under their own brand names.

Further, not all ORS is suitable for diarrhoea in children. Electral, for instance, was the leading brand in India, the name used almost as a generic, but it was not intended for this purpose. It was as likely as not that a customer asking for ORS would ask for it by that name; or, asking by the generic name, would be given Electral, which was not meant for infantile diarrhoea. (In the Hindi-speaking markets of North India, the common way to refer to ORS was *ghol*.)

The correct product is a WHO-recommended formulation (which for brevity we will call WHO ORS) designed for this purpose with the right ingredients in the right proportions. It was absolutely critical that both the customer and the chemist be able to easily identify the WHO-recommended product, whatever its brand name or the packaging it was in. It was not important that they know why that was the right one; only that it was. How could we help the consumer identify and pick up the right one? To list all the brands in communications, in the hope that she would remember and ask for it by name, would have been wishful thinking.

The solution seems self-evident in hindsight. A graphic was created, featuring an infant, to identify the WHO-recommended formulation. Manufacturers of WHO ORS were lobbied to carry the graphic on their packaging and promotional material. We told them we were going to spend a large sum of money promoting that symbol, and offered them the opportunity to carry it on their packs. Of course they saw the sense of doing so, given that they could then benefit from a fairly large communications programme to which that graphic would be quite central. Thus, every pack of WHO ORS carried the identifying symbol, so the customer could tell it was the right one, whatever the brand name; and so, of course, did all the communication. This single, simple piece was in a sense the underpinning of the entire exercise, without which the whole programme could have been infructuous.

## Mass Media Advertising

Television was the single medium, running one TV ad targeted at mothers. The key message was that WHO ORS is much more effective than traditional home remedies and is recommended by doctors.

## Public Relations

The programme was launched at a press conference in Delhi, followed by Bhopal, Patna, Lucknow and Jaipur, to highlight the danger of diarrhoea in children and the effectiveness, ease, economy and availability of WHO ORS. A series of relevant articles were placed in local and regional media, on diarrhoea, its causes, and management, highlighting WHO ORS as a solution.

About 438 newspaper articles appeared, including 226 health articles, 61 covering the national launch conference, 148 on state level conferences, and 3 one-on-one meetings with editors.

## Partnerships and Tie-ups

Balaji Telefilms, producers of several leading TV serials, agreed to feature key campaign messages in one of the episodes of the top TV soap opera of the day, *Kyunki Saas Bhi Kabhi Bahu Thi*. A situation was scripted into the serial in which a doctor talking to the two leading female characters, Baa and Tulsi, recommends WHO ORS for a child suffering from diarrhoea!

In a partnership with Hindustan Lever, posters were designed, which talked about the use of ORS in diarrhoea and about prevention of diarrhoea by washing hands with Lifebuoy soap.

Subsequent such partnership included those with Star TV, Zee TV, Sony TV, Sahara TV, PVR Cinemas, UTI Bank, Mother Dairy and Delhi Transport Corporation.

## Direct Contact

Direct contact was a key component of the programme, targeting the three key audiences with messages relevant to each.

In year one, demonstrations were organised in Delhi and select cities of Uttar Pradesh for groups of mothers of children below five years of age. They were encouraged to use WHO ORS in every episode of diarrhoea and were also educated about the importance of correct preparation and of keeping the product at home.

In partnership with the Indian Academy of Paediatrics (IAP), mailers were sent to doctors, enlisting their support in preventing millions of deaths every year that are due to dehydration in diarrhoea. The mailer advised them to prescribe WHO ORS in every episode of diarrhoea in children. This mailer came from their professional body and promoted no brand. That gave the programme a stamp of authority far removed from the commercial messages doctors are exposed to all the time.

Field teams visited 60,000 chemists and ISMPs at least three times during the year to ensure that they recommended or dispensed WHO ORS in every episode of diarrhoea.

To induce chemists to stock and recommend WHO ORS, a mystery consumer contest was designed. Chemists were briefed about the upcoming contest and participants were enlisted. Field workers posing as customers visited participating outlets and checked the responses on three identified parameters. Chemists who scored on all three parameters won prizes. Of the 11,500 chemists who participated in the contest, 4,800 gave the correct answers and won prizes. WHO ORS was available in 55% of outlets, against 23% in the previous year.

## ORS Day

To drive peak attention levels at the right time, 29 July was designated as the National ORS Day, and has been observed every year since then. At the end of July, when the monsoon is at its peak in North India, there is an increase in the number of diarrhoea cases.

Numerous events and tie-ups were organised for the occasion, with accompanying press coverage. Seminars, rallies and product demonstrations were run all over the target markets. The Indian Academy of Paediatrics lent its support through events organised by its local chapters.

## Sales Results

Very few social marketing programmes set and monitor targets for outcomes, whether sales or any other: this one did. That is the right thing to do, as only then do you know whether the programme achieved what it set out to.

The target for the first year of the programme was 11% growth in consumer offtake of the category as a whole and 14% in WHO ORS. By the end of the year, while total ORS grew by 17% over the previous year, WHO ORS grew by 45%.[21] This suggested that the programme had been able to distinguish quite sharply between the two, and guide customers to the right product.

## Follow Through

Taking stock of the first year of the programme, it appeared that while promoting ORS as the first response in diarrhoea remained the primary communication task, it was also very important to make target groups aware of the importance of correct preparation.

Compliance is a key issue in healthcare marketing. Patients and caregivers often tend to either overdose or under-dose, and increase or decrease the frequency, according to their judgment.

21 ORG Retail Audit

If the treatment is ineffective or there are side effects, the fault is usually assigned to the treatment—or to the doctor! In the current instance, we found mothers were using less than required.

### *Mass media*

A new TV ad was developed, the message of which was that preparing WHO ORS correctly was as important as giving it in every episode of diarrhoea. As there was specific information to communicate, print supplemented TV, with an ad running in women's magazines.

### *Public relations*

The emphasis of the public relations programme too shifted. The primary message in articles, media briefings and editor meetings was the importance of correct preparation. Local medical professionals were co-opted to give advice in local media. Around 239 articles appeared, including 78 health articles, 102 reports of ORS day events, 36 on media meetings, and 11 one-on-one meetings with editors.

In a continuation of the previous year's association, Balaji Telefilms once again included a segment on *Kyunki Saas Bhi Kabhi Bahu Thi* on Star Plus. In this episode Tulsi and Baa are in a clinic, viewing the correct preparation of WHO ORS demonstrated by a doctor!

Star Plus and Zee TV also aired short information spots between programmes, with key campaign messages.

### *Direct contact*

The highlight of the direct contact programme was a team of trained promoters calling door-to-door on 77,000 mothers with children under five years of age. They explained the dangers of diarrhoea and the importance of WHO ORS, and gave a step-by-step demonstration of the correct preparation. In each home, they left behind a sample pack of WHO ORS and a leaflet.

According to an ORG prescription audit at the time, ISMPs treated almost 42% of all children below two years of age suffering from diarrhoea, but only one in fourteen of their prescriptions was for WHO ORS. CMS teams detailed and provided campaign materials to 60,000 ISMPs in 500 cities and towns in the target markets. A special programme called 'Gift a Life' was mounted for them, in which an ISMP who prescribed WHO ORS was given a personalised certificate to display.

## Programme Results

Over the two years, consumer offtake of WHO ORS in the target markets grew by 82%, in the rest of India by 38%. The difference showed this was not natural market growth but programme-induced. Also, while WHO ORS grew by 82% in the target markets, regular (non-WHO) ORS grew by 24%.[22] Again, this difference showed that the programme had succeeded in establishing the critical fact that all ORS are not the same.

The programme was clearly on the right track. Seeing the results of the two-year effort, USAID and ICICI Bank decided to extend it.

## Year Three

What was now needed was the continuation of the theme message with the diarrhoea-dehydration-WHO ORS story, and the promotion of stocking the product at home so that it was available at hand whenever diarrhoea struck.

### *Mass media*

Two new TV ads were created: a fresh one for the 'theme' message and one to underscore the importance of keeping a pack at home.

22 ORG Retail Audit

### *Public relations*

In-serial promotions were worked out with Star Plus, Zee TV and Sony TV. Channel fillers with celebrity endorsement were created and aired by Sahara TV.

CMS teams organised a range of activities in thirty-four key cities with coverage in more than 100 publications and several TV stations.

### *Direct contact*

In a repetition of the previous year's programme, promoters met 200,000 mothers in door-to-door visits.

CMS staff called on 28,000 ISMPs and 28,000 chemists. Each partner manufacturer's medical representatives detailed 9,000 doctors.

## Long-term Effects

Partner manufacturers saw commercial gains from WHO ORS, encouraging and enabling them to increase their marketing support. Seeing the market opportunity, many more manufacturers started making WHO ORS, and the combined efforts of an increased number of manufacturers further accelerated the adoption of this critical practice.

The Indian Academy of Paediatrics convened a special task force to review the guidelines for diarrhoea management in children. The recommendation of the task force was formally endorsed by the Academy and conveyed to the Ministry of Health and Family Welfare, and the Drug Controller of India. Consequently, the new, more effective low osmolarity WHO-recommended formula was adopted by the Government of India and included in the Indian Pharmacopoeia. That means that as it is the only ORS formula in India, all ORS is now equal.

## Lessons from the Programme

The success of the programme demonstrates the need to integrate the essential components of a behaviour change campaign, especially behaviour in which the key target audience has high stakes.

### *Saying the right thing to the right person*

The programme identified all constituents involved in the process. It identified the crucial messages required to encourage trial and use, and focused on the different stages of the behaviour change process—from informing non-users to convincing potential users and retaining and reinforcing current users. While doing so, it carried all the relevant constituents along.

### *Balanced and consistent communication*

This was a well-modulated campaign that used an even balance of messages that percolated down to the right target groups and were converted into action. All elements of the communications programme—mass media advertising, public relations, and outreach—delivered the same message. At each stage, the key messages changed according to market need, but all elements of the communication mix were consistent in what they delivered.

### *Leveraging media*

The programme worked closely with media partners, with messages calibrated at each stage. The public relations programme extended the reach and frequency of advertising messages and added the credibility and authority of the press to the communication.

### *Leveraging ground events*

Ground events are very good for involving the audience, but obviously have limited reach. To get the full value for the time, effort and money spent on it, an event must be reported in the relevant mass media so that its message reaches many more people than those present at it. An event where a few hundred were present can reach tens of thousands, at little or no cost. And, oh yes, in what is said and how it is said, the event must be made worthy of reporting.

### *Partnerships work*

A number of partnerships were forged and developed across the years, and added immeasurably to the programme—IAP, Balaji Telefilms, Star TV, Zee TV, Sony TV, Sahara TV, Delhi Transport Corporation, Mother Dairy, UTI Bank, WHO ORS manufacturers—and the unique strength of each partner was leveraged.

### *Building coalitions*

In social marketing, in particular, you will find that there are government bodies, industry bodies, and NGOs that share your agenda. Sometimes it just isn't as high up in their priorities as it is in yours, but they are open to supporting you. Sometimes they don't have the resources to do what they want to, and welcome your support and at other times they are doing a good job already and are happy to welcome you to the fold. Identify them and build lasting coalitions with them. These are not transactional relationships: once they adopt your agenda and fold it into theirs, they will continue to promote it.

# CHAPTER 6
# What Went Wrong with Tata Nano?*

When the Tata Nano was unveiled, the Haves groaned.

The triumphant arrival in January 2008 of the much-awaited 'People's Car' was hailed around the world, but Indian car owners were not amused. They blanched at the prospect of those cheap little buggies breeding like cockroaches, jamming the already-overcrowded roads, and wished Ratan Tata had left the Great Unwashed to their own devices.

Soon after came the crisis in Singur; then building the plant at Sanand, with limited supplies coming out of temporary facilities; and finally, in June 2010, production commenced at the new 250,000-a-year plant. At last, enough for everyone.

But the People sat on their hands. You did not need data to see that something was not quite as expected, but the data supported what you thought you saw: sales dropped steadily month-by-month, from 9,000 in July of the year to 3,000 in October, even as the passenger car market in the country was surging.

What was the matter?

It was not the product. It was spacious (I'm six feet, three inches tall, and I drove it comfortably); the air-conditioning was quick and effective even in the Delhi summer; at 60 kmph it drove

* Enlarged and updated from my original article, 'I'm too sexy for my shoes,' published in *Campaign India*, December 2010.

effortlessly and sat snugly on the road; it parked like a dream and sipped fuel delicately. And all that for ₹ 1.70 lakh. Yes, not the touted ₹ 1 lakh, but by far the cheapest car in the country, and superb value by any measure. It was, in fact, my preferred car if I was driving myself to dinner and had to park in a typically crowded South Delhi colony or at a restaurant. With no power steering and thinly padded seats it was of course not as comfortable to drive as my other cars, but it was fun.

Don't take my word for it. Hormazd Sorabjee, editor of *Autocar India* and the country's leading auto journalist, described it like this: 'For a car that weighs a mere 600kg, the Nano feels incredibly robust. You expect the doors to rattle, the seats to squeak and those dinner-plate-sized wheels to buckle driving over rough Indian roads. But instead, the Nano feels rigid, well screwed together, and deftly darts from one pothole to another with ease. The suspension copes with any sort of surface and the Nano's massive ground clearance can shame some off-roaders.'[23]

Nor was it the want of availability: I got mine in four days. I was glad for that, but it also meant, in a burgeoning car market, that even in those early days of Nano not enough people wanted one. You may blame limited supply for the low on-the-road numbers, but if a product is available off the shelf despite limited supply, clearly there isn't enough demand.

The trouble was that it was cool: way too cool.

Nano was a proud symbol of contemporary India: not just standing toe-to-toe with the world, but teaching it a thing or two. It was not cheap and nasty, it was cheap and cheerful and a product not of *jugaad*, but of technological innovation. *The Economic Times* reported then that the 67,000 Nano owners at the time included 'corporate chieftains who otherwise ride on cars whose four wheels alone could buy the people's car'. To Nano

23 Hormazd Sorabjee, 'Nano: Triumph of Indian ingenuity', BBC News, 23 March 2009, http://news.bbc.co.uk/2/hi/south_asia/7958498.stm.

owners like me this was an affirmation, and strengthened positive feelings about the car; to those considering it for a second or third car, it was another nudge in that direction. And the car certainly turned heads. At the traffic lights, at a petrol bunk or in a parking lot people looked at it with interest, and often came up to take a look inside and ask questions.

Marketing people would give their eye teeth to get their brand such a cachet. But Nano had become the rich man's toy, to be bought on a whim, instead of a real car for real, hard-working middle-class families taking out a loan to get one. It didn't even look like a real car—funny shape, no bonnet and no boot. In a market accustomed to hatchbacks, it didn't even have a hatch.

The problem, though, was not what it was or how it looked: it was that Tata Motors did not control the communication and manage expectations.

The press reportage was so overwhelming and so positive that it was perhaps tempting to think it was enough and more. But the press did what they should have done, which was to be excited about Ratan Tata's vision and its realisation; the innovative technology; national pride; and, of course, the Singur fracas and its aftermath. They reported the scepticism of auto manufacturers around the world, who were scoffing at the idea of the 'one-lakh-rupee car', with Carlos Ghosn of Renault Nissan the sole believer, and rooted for Tata and India. They speculated about the price tag: would it, wouldn't it be the magic figure? What they did not do was to fire the aspiration of the family on the scooter that inspired the vision, and assure them that this little marvel was a safe, reliable, economical car for them—nor was it their job to do so. That was the job of the marketer, who failed completely at it.

March 2009 saw the commercial launch of the car. Anticipating huge demand, Tata Motors announced that they would allocate cars by lottery. They had a shade over two lakh bookings, and the first Nano was delivered in July 2009.

The first TV commercial, at the end of 2010, was addressed to the first-time car buyer. At about the same time, Tata Motors launched a two-wheeler exchange scheme. But they were marketing to someone who had never bought a car, and had probably never before thought they ever could. Think about it: in the socio-cultural environment of India, how likely was that middle-class family on the scooter to walk into a car showroom and ask to see cars? About as likely as they were to walk into a Rolex showroom. They would expect at least to be ignored, probably to be rebuffed.

If the customer won't come to the product, take the product to the customer. That is what Tata Motors did, or perhaps thought they were doing. What they did do was to put Nano on display at Westside and Croma stores. The stores took bookings, and sold Nano merchandise such as baseball caps and T-shirts. Both those retail chains belong to Tata, but that has nothing to do with the customer. If you were thinking of the customer, how likely were you to pick Westside and Croma as locations to reach two-wheeler upgraders? And why would anyone have paid to own Nano-branded apparel?

Sales continued to drop, to about 550 units in December 2010 (from 9,000 in July and 3,000 in October), six months after the brand-new Sanand factory commenced production.

By March 2011 Tata Motors went finally to where their customers were, by tying up with Big Bazaar to do what they had been doing at Westside and Croma. Too little, too late. They also opened several hundred kiosks around the country, but only in remote areas where they had no dealership, with a view to extending their network. In urban areas, where the market for cars is, they did nothing.

Meanwhile, State Bank of India, with which Tata had an exclusive arrangement, began to advertise auto loans for Nano.

The protagonist was a city bus driver, driving a Nano to work: not quite an aspirational role model for middle-class families.

That was reminiscent of Air Deccan, in its original avatar, the first budget airline in India. Launched in 2003 with the promise 'Now everyone can fly', it grew within two years from a fleet of two ATR-42 turboprop aircraft to thirty, including the Airbus A-320, flying trunk routes through the country. In 2005, having built capacity, they began to advertise on television. In the commercial, titled 'The Old Man and the Sky' the protagonist was a village carpenter taking a flight for the first time. 'Heart-tugging performances and breath-taking cinematography are highlights of the film,' said a company statement. Lovely, but what did it do for the brand? To whom was the ad addressed, and for whom was it making the airline aspirational? What it probably did do—purely in my judgement, based on anecdotal evidence—was to tell many of those who had started travelling by it that Air Deccan was not quite the place to be seen in.

'Along with TV, internet is also one of the lead mediums to build reach,' reported afaqs.com, a trade website. 'The commercial will be put exclusively on Indiatimes.com. Soon after the TV premiere, people can log onto Air Deccan's website and answer a few simple questions. The prize? The correct/selected entries will win 250 return tickets for the fathers of the participants.'[24] Good thinking, with TV and the internet working together and bringing the commercial to life—but for whom?

Coming back to Nano, either the State Bank commercial had Tata Motors' approval, or it did not and they allowed it to run: unforgivable, either way.

Over the next few years the car went through several upgrades.

24 'The Old Man & the Sky: Air Deccan's latest 150-second innovation,' afaqs.com, 7 July 2005, http://www.afaqs.com/news/story/11974_The-Old-Man--the-Sky-Air-Deccans-latest-150-sec-innovation.

In 2012 the seats and the suspension were improved, making the ride more comfortable; the engine power was increased slightly and the gearing was modified to improve fuel economy; and there were some cosmetic changes like beige interiors and covering the exposed seat rails. With that came advertising that featured young people—college kids, from the look of them—having fun: first-time car owners, but hardly in the mainstream. To its credit, though, the commercial did attempt to describe and demonstrate the key features of the car: spaciousness, ground clearance, air-conditioning, and fuel efficiency.

In 2013 there were some small changes, like a larger steering wheel to (hopefully) make up for the absence of power steering and the addition of some chrome on the exteriors. The advertising was more of the same, or perhaps less of the same: it continued to present Nano as young and cool, featuring an age profile slightly older than the college kids of the previous ad, but did away with anything to do with functionality. There was just a lot of singing and dancing, ending with a series of tag lines: 'Celebrate Youness; Celebrate Kickassness; Celebrate Epicness; Celebrate Magicness; Celebrate Awesomeness.' I cite those lines only to show, by the language, how far Nano had come from where it started.

In subsequent upgrades came power steering, keyless entry, Bluetooth connectivity, Automated Manual Transmission (AMT) and an openable hatch and, of course, several cosmetic changes alongside.

But all that did nothing for sales. From a peak of over 74,000 units in the financial year 2011–12, sales dropped precipitously to 1,851 units in the financial year 2017–18. In June 2018 the company sold just three units, and made only one. There is some talk of a Nano-based electric vehicle being developed for Ola Cabs, but it is clearly the end of the road for Nano as it was envisioned, turning from a dream to the dust of reality in ten years.

In those few years the advertising changed dramatically, seeming to successively target audiences that were polar opposites; and distribution seemed to have a mind of its own, unconnected and unconcerned with who the prospective buyer was.

'A cheap car that's not really cheap. A safe car whose safety has been questioned. A poor people's car that poor people aren't buying. That sounds like a failure, certainly,' wrote Matt Eyring, a strategy innovation consultant.[25] 'But really it's not. It's par for the course for almost every breakthrough innovation. There's nothing unusual about a company having to adjust the price, the production process, the marketing, or even the market of a breakthrough offering... In fact, I can think of only one example of a CEO who pre-announced an innovation that was going to change the world and actually delivered it. That's Steve Jobs, of course.' The real problem, said Eyring, was 'the hype surrounding it that tied Tata's hands'.

To start with, Nano received an overwhelming amount of the wrong sort of publicity. Yes, there is such a thing as too much communication. Tags like 'one-lakh-rupee car' and 'the world's cheapest car' made good copy for the media, and kept the car in the public eye, an object of curiosity, but not necessarily desirable to the intended buyer.

With all that publicity, everything about the development of Nano was in the public gaze. Thus every development was publicly examined and critiqued, with opinions weighing in for and against. The 'one-lakh-rupee' price was discussed endlessly. On the one hand, every product development was hailed in the media as a breakthrough; on the other, it was called out as a tacit admission that the product had not been up to scratch. Nano was getting dressed in a glass house with the lights on and the world outside watching. Tata Motors didn't intend it that way, but it was

25 Mat Eyring, 'Learning from Tata's Nano Mistakes,' Harvard Business Review, 11 January 2011, https://hbr.org/2011/01/learning-from-tatas-nano-mista.

a fact of life: the media were moulding public opinion and Tata Motors were not controlling the communication.

'It might not have been easy, but had Tata piloted the Nano quietly, on a small scale, perhaps through a limited production run in a small city like Durgapur in West Bengal or Ranchi in Jharkand, its engineering, pricing, financing, and marketing might have been adjusted far from the limelight to suit the needs of an optimal target customer,' wrote Eyring. 'It might not have been a 1 lakh car or even an alternative to motor scooters. But when it first appeared in the mainstream, it would have been the right product for the right price in the right market.'

# CHAPTER 7
# A Service Is Not a Product*

After weeks of resistance I succumbed to the iPad. The argument against it was that there aren't many Wi-Fi hotspots in India, which limits your ability to use one. The answer was to get the one with 3G. That's not central to this story; it is only to say why I was in the market for a mobile phone connection.

Well, Saturday was Christmas and I was going to be travelling from Monday, and you know how it is with tech toys: I wasn't going to wait until I returned and went to my office. And so it came to pass that on the Sunday after Christmas I was shopping for a mobile connection.

I chose Airtel, unsurprisingly perhaps, given the 3G options available and the recent salience of the brand.

From the website I got a list of outlets within a short radius of my home. It gave addresses and had columns for parking ('Yes' for all), timing (10am to 8pm for all), and the weekly day off (blank for all), but, strangely for a telecom company, no telephone numbers.

I have Airtel landlines and ADSL at home and some kind of preferred customer status, so I called the designated customer service number. After wading through the interactive voice

---

* Adapted and enlarged from my original January 2011 blog with the same title.

response (IVR) menu and getting a live human voice at the other end (Why do call centres speak to you in Hindi after you press '1' for English?), I was told this number was only for landlines and that I should call 98101 98101.

So I did. When I asked where I should go for a new connection, the gent said, 'You can get it where you buy recharge coupons.'

'Ah, but I don't buy recharge coupons,' I replied. 'I need to get a mobile connection first.'

'I'm trying to help you,' he said. 'If you don't find that helpful there's not much I can do,' and hung up. Being well trained, though, he didn't forget to first say, 'Thank you for calling Airtel.'

I stubbornly called again and got someone else. She said that number was only for prepaid connections: for 'postpaid', as the term goes, I should call 98100 12345.

So I did. More IVR, about bill payment and value-added services and so forth, and 'to go back to the main menu press 1', or whatever. Oh, I missed what I needed. Back to the main menu. But I was right the first time: every conceivable kind of information was available except if you wanted a new connection.

Clearly, Airtel didn't expect that if you wanted a new telephone connection you might use a telephone to help get one.

I got that list from the website and set out.

The first outlet was closed. And the second. And the third...'*Aaj* Sunday *hai na, ji* (It's Sunday, you see)'. If the website hadn't left the thoughtful 'weekly off' column thoughtlessly blank, or had given a phone number to call, I would have saved time and trouble. (It was right about parking, though, when it said 'Yes': after all, there was a street outside each outlet.)

Four phone calls and an outing later, I was no closer to a mobile connection.

Here is a company at the top of the heap; grown in hardly twenty years from small beginnings to a name to reckon with internationally; grown from selling cheap Chinese telephone instruments to mobile telephony to fixed-line telephony, broadband internet, IPTV and DTH. A single brand, a single website—but not a single phone number.

Why would someone doing business in the twenty-first century and listing outlets, not give their phone numbers?

What does it take for a telecom company to think of having a universal toll-free phone number that anyone wishing to buy its services can call, to be directed by an IVR system to what they are looking for?

Mass market services are often equated with fast-moving consumer goods (FMCG), and services referred to as products. Years ago that not only sounded sexy, but also brought attention to the idea that a service had to be taken out to the user, not wait for the user to come to it, as had largely been the case in India. Now it only distracts attention from the fact that there is more to mass market services than making them available 'within an arm's reach of desire'.[26]

For FMCG, the store is essentially a stocking point. Its overriding role is to provide convenient access, and anyone going to any store gets the standardised product. The task of marketing is essentially to make the product available and desirable, and the brand experience lies in ownership and usage. It doesn't matter where you buy a bar of soap or a shampoo or cooking oil: your feelings about it are not affected by the state of the shop or if the fellow who sold it to you was surly. The brand is delivered by the physical attributes of the product, combined with the mental connections you make around it.

Mass market services, on the other hand, are largely invisible and undifferentiated in use. It is in the interaction—at the bank counter, at the store, on the telephone or on the internet—that the

26 The phrase is attributed to Robert Woodruff, President of The Coca-Cola Company from 1923 to 1954. It was his vision 'to put Coca-Cola within an arm's reach of desire'.

brand is delivered by the teller, the sales assistant, the call centre operator or the guy who does all the boring detail on the website.

Marketers of products experience what they and their competitors sell. They compare products, in use as well as technically; and routinely visit retail outlets. But marketers of services typically don't. As a marketer of services, unless you call the toll-free number or customer service, or transact on the internet or at the counter, you will never know how your customer receives your brand. You will not know what they experience when their telephone line is down, or when their credit card transaction is not approved.

With growing competition and increasingly exposed consumers, the quality of products from cars to candy is, over the last several years, benchmarked globally; but that of mass market services is still benchmarked locally. It's a circular relationship: customers' expectations of services are limited by what they experience—shaped largely, perhaps, by the standards of the largest service provider, the government—and the services they get only cater to their low expectations.

## ...But a Product Is Often a Service

'People don't buy products, they buy the expectation of benefits,' said Norman Berry, former Creative Director of Ogilvy & Mather. 'No one wants a quarter-inch drill bit,' he said, 'they want a quarter-inch hole. And if that's what they want, a half-inch drill bit won't do.'

The same is true of most durables. No one needs a refrigerator, for example. They want to preserve food and cool water, and the product is only a delivery system for that benefit. Delivery of uninterrupted service must be at the heart of marketing durables.

In a very different space, Anil Gore, former Managing Director of *Reader's Digest*, once told me, 'We are not in the publishing business. We are in a reader service business. We first find out what kind of content you want to read. We then scour the world to find material that we think would be of interest to you. From that we select a range of material to cater to the interests of the whole family. We edit abridge, and put it into an easy-to-read form. Then we compile it into a handy volume, and deliver it at your door once a month.' That attitude, that approach, has kept *Reader's Digest* going for nearly a 100 years.

Not so long ago, petrol bunks were shabby, quite dirty places. All the oil-marketing companies, as they are called, were government-owned and prices were government controlled, and you couldn't tell one from another.

In the mid-1990s, the then Chairman of Bharat Petroleum asked me one day what his company should do to be competitive. I recalled Anil Gore and *Reader's Digest.*

You are not in the business of refining and distributing petroleum products, I told him. You are in the business of delivering services in relation to petroleum products.

Your petrol, diesel and lubricants are not different from or better than those of HP or Indian Oil. The three of you have refineries in different places and buy from each other, so you sell the exact same products. And if they are in some way different and deliver a slightly different performance, you can't commit that and the customer can't make it out because, in the end, performance is a function of vehicle, road, load, and driving conditions.

But look at it this way. I need fuel for my car. You make it conveniently available, close to wherever I am. I simply drive in, someone fills it while I keep sitting comfortably in my car, and I carry on. Again, I need fuel to cook. You process gas, pack it in a safe cylinder, and deliver it at my door. One phone call is all it takes. You also help to make sure I can use it. If there is a leak, if the pipe needs replacing, if there is a problem with my stove, one phone call and your man is there to fix it.

That's service, and that is the business you are in. The more convenient and pleasant you can make that experience, the more you will have me choosing Bharat Petroleum over your competition. Give me a reason to go up the road and make a U-turn to go to your outlet instead of to HP on this side of the road.

# CHAPTER 8
# Your Company Is Also a Brand

**'Eighty-one out of the hundred biggest American corporations advertise their corporations, as distinct from their products, and spend $500,000,000 a year in the process. Most of them make a hash of it.'**

***—David Ogilvy***

*Ogilvy on Adverstising, 1983*

The multidimensionality of brands acquires an even larger significance when you consider a company as a brand. The implication is more obvious in the case of a company like IBM, which is the name of the company as well as that by which its products and services are distinguished; or a group like Tata, which uses the same name for many of its companies as well as its products and services across business and categories. Less obvious, perhaps, is the case of companies like Hindustan Unilever and ITC, which do not use the company name for their products and services. But the company too is a brand, in many markets: the stock market and the employment market, to name but two.

This thought was expounded by Philip Kotler nearly fifty years ago[27]—long before the term 'integrated marketing communications' came into being. The essence of Kotler's thesis, expanding on the then relatively recent concept of marketing, was that a corporation deals with a number of what he called 'publics', and must market to each of them. The nature of the corporation's relationships with its publics varies, and so accordingly do their expectations of it. Equally important, these publics—or markets—do interact with each other as well, not only in the context of the corporation but otherwise, and influence each other, and sometimes their interests are in conflict.

Consider the case of a company that, to support its profitability, closes down a plant employing 5,000 people. That act in the interest of its investors works directly against the interests of the affected employees and of vendors (though it may work in favour of employees of other plants, who get to keep their jobs, by strengthening the company), and possibly of the local government and community. The media by their reportage influence how the employees, the government and the community feel about the closure; special interest groups may take a position on the matter and influence the media and, therefore, other markets; investors react to public opinion by investing or divesting in shares; the trade and vendors may begin to feel insecure about their own future business with the corporation; and, of course, the corporation's customers, who live in the same environment and are subject to the same influences, form opinions about the corporation relative to its competition; and intending buyers may drop the company's products from consideration.

27 Philip Kotler, 'A Generic Concept of Marketing,' *Journal of Marketing* 36, no. 2 (April 1972): pp. 46–54.

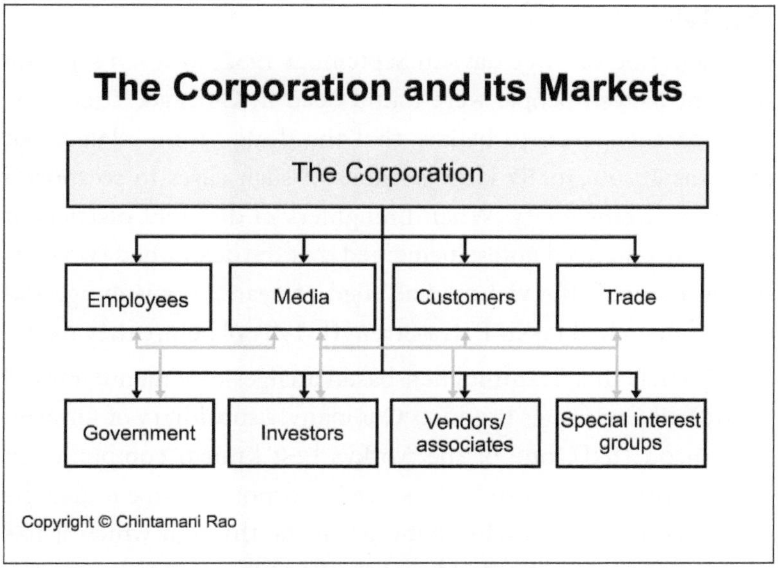


**Figure 8.1: The Corporation and Its Markets**

*Source*: Author

This is obviously more of an issue in a bad news situation rather than when the corporation is taking positive action. Public relations consultants across the world advise their clients in crisis preparedness; and it is good to be prepared, but credibility cannot be bought overnight. At such times there is no better defence than the corporation's own brand equity, its reputation nurtured over time. Indeed, a crisis situation is the stress test for corporate communications and for the corporate brand—for crises will occur—the question is what you do and how your publics respond, when they do.

The event that perhaps best illustrates this is one that made history in many different ways.

## The Tylenol Crisis

Over a period of three days in September 1982, in seven separate incidents, seven people were found dead in Chicago. There was no apparent reason to believe that the deaths were related, but that was an unusually large number of such cases in so short a period in a single city. When firefighters in different districts of Chicago exchanged notes, it emerged that the deaths had two facts in common: all the victims had died of cyanide poisoning, and each of them had taken Extra-Strength Tylenol before they died.

Tylenol, an acetaminophen-based analgesic, is manufactured by McNeil Consumer Products Company, a subsidiary of Johnson & Johnson (J&J), one of the world's best known companies in healthcare and baby products (since its corporate name is also the brand name of its flagship baby products, through which it has been known to, and trusted by, generations of mothers around the world).

Launched in 1960 as a safe substitute for aspirin, Tylenol was by 1981 the leading analgesic in the US market. At the time of this crisis it was contributing 8% of the sales of J&J and was their most profitable product.

The first, obvious, conclusion from the deaths in Chicago was that, one way or the other, the product was contaminated during manufacture. But it turned out that the poisoned bottles not only were from different lots but also came from two different plants. The authorities were satisfied that whatever might have happened, it did not happen at J&J's facilities.

The scale of the media coverage this tragedy received is best described by two indicators. The first, that according to one estimate it had the widest domestic media coverage of any story since the assassination of President Kennedy; and the second, a study conducted by the company that said more than 90% of Americans knew about the Tylenol-related deaths within the first week of the crisis. Competitors were quick to respond: promoting non-aspirin products; stressing tamper-proof packaging; and advancing planned product launches to fill the gap created by the sudden demise of the market leader.

The immediate business implications for J&J were, clearly, that Tylenol was as good as dead and, of course, that the company would suffer a huge loss in consequence.

'I don't think they can ever sell another product under that name,' said Jerry Della Femina, an eminent advertising man, to the *The New York Times*. 'There may be an advertising person who thinks he can solve this, and if they find him I want to hire him because then I want him to turn our water cooler into a wine cooler.'[28]

Della Femina was, typically, thinking advertising. J&J were not. What followed was not just a textbook case in crisis management: it wrote the textbook. In fact, there are those who would have it that the very practice of crisis preparedness started with the Tylenol incident.

Instead of locking themselves in and putting the lights out until the storm blew over; instead of putting up defences against the onslaught and looking for scapegoats; instead of engaging in obfuscation, jargon and diplomatese, J&J did exactly the opposite: opened up all manner of communication channels. Against government advice,[29] they recalled thirty-one million bottles of Tylenol, at a cost of $50 million; proactively and promptly put out accurate information to the press; sent 500,000 mailgrams to doctors and hospitals and 150,000 to distributors and retailers, notifying them of the contamination. The company's CEO, James Burke, went repeatedly on television to answer questions; they established toll-free phone lines for the public to call in; and even

28 Quoted by Tamara Kaplan in 'The Tylenol Crisis: How Effective Public Relations Saved Johnson & Johnson', *The Pennsylvania State University*, http://www.personal.psu.edu/users/w/x/wxk116/tylenol/crisis.

29 The FDA feared that a recall would worsen the panic caused by the deaths; and the FBI, that it would show how easily terrorists could bring a multibillion-dollar corporation to its knees.

sent two rounds of communication to current employees as well as retirees to keep them informed about what their company was doing in that difficult situation.

In market research surveys prior to the poisonings, less than 1% of customers were found to have been aware that J&J was the company behind Tylenol. After the incident, more than 45% were. Far from distancing itself from the tragedy, J&J actually identified itself with it. And though 87% of respondents felt the company was not responsible for the deaths, 61% said they were unlikely to purchase Extra-Strength Tylenol capsules in the future.

Within ten weeks of the recall, J&J began putting Extra-Strength Tylenol back on the shelves in new, tamper-resistant packaging. This was supported by several communication initiatives targeted at consumers, the trade, as well as the medical community. In time Tylenol, pronounced as good as dead, won back consumer confidence and 95% of the market share it had prior to the poisonings.[30]

## The Strength of the Corporate Brand

The Tylenol case is taught and cited in management and public relations courses, and wherever crisis management and corporate image management are discussed, as the gold standard. What it is not so often seen as is a case in corporate brand management and, indeed, in the rewards of effective management of the corporate brand.

That the response of the J&J management was exemplary from the standpoint of both social responsibility and public relations is inarguable. But what the company did could only be as effective as the credence given to it by its constituent markets or publics. That, in turn, is a function of the equity of the corporate brand. That was the single most powerful and valuable asset the management

30 Who was behind the Tylenol poisoning and how it was effected was never found.

of J&J had, going into the crisis, and it was not merely fortuitous but had been carefully and deliberately built over time.

In the mid-1940s Robert Wood Johnson, son of the company's founder and its leader for fifty years, wrote a simple, four-paragraph credo defining the company's responsibility to its constituencies. That has since adorned every facility of the company and the office of every one of its executives; forms the bedrock of its corporate culture; and guides its operations, policies and decisions. Robert Johnson was thinking of corporate social responsibility, in doing which too he was ahead of his times, but what he did in the process was to define the Johnson & Johnson brand.

The management's response to the Tylenol crisis was the corporate brand's trial by fire. Because the management lived the brand and walked the talk, their reflex response was consistent with the values and architecture of the brand. 'Later we realised that no meeting had been called to make the first critical decision: to be open with the press and put the consumer interest first,' reported Lawrence Foster, Corporate Vice President of public relations. In his article, Foster quotes Burke as saying, 'Every one of us knew what we had to do. There was no need to meet. We had the credo philosophy to guide us.'[31]

This was corporate brand management at its best. Here was a company conscious that while it deals with many constituencies through many different points of contact, it itself is a single whole.[32]

This story also illustrates how all communications from and about a company are linked. A company actively puts out communications of various kinds: advertising to consumers, its annual report to investors, internal news and policy

31 Lawrence G Foster, 'The Johnson & Johnson Credo and the Tylenol Crisis', *New Jersey Bell Journal* 6, no. 1 (1983).

32 In recent years, J&J has been under fire in the US with users of Johnson's Baby Powder claiming that asbestos in the talc had caused ovarian cancer; and in India with patients claiming that its hip implants were faulty. The company is fighting protracted battles on both issues. Who is right in either case is not for us to say, but what is clear is that J&J is on the losing side on the PR front. That is ironic, coming from the company that successfully navigated a crisis of epochal proportions.

announcements, press releases, speeches by its executives and so on. The audiences such communications reaches are not faceless, discrete monoliths: each of them is made up of living, breathing human beings, many of whom belong to two or more audiences. After all, shareholders buy products, employees read newspapers and watch television, and doctors have families who have headaches and colds and use medicine to treat them, like everyone else.

Many companies have corporate communications departments, and many more still put out what are called corporate campaigns: advertisements extolling the virtues of the company, typically put out prior to an IPO or any event for which the company wants to quickly marshal public opinion in its favour.

Thus, corporate image management is typically a series of activities designed and executed as and when needed, to meet the management's desire to connect with particular audiences at particular times—most often with investors and governments—and put out messages for them. For shareholders it is about financial results; for dealers, return on investment; for employees, compensation and career prospects; and for government, either about policy or about that delightful term 'contribution to the exchequer', which makes paying taxes sound like magnanimity. Rarely does a company define its persona as a whole, lay down its guiding principles clearly and publicly for all to see and know, and live by them, as J&J did.

## What Goes Wrong with Corporate Communications?

Most corporate campaigns are short-lived because they don't have a clear purpose to start with. Except when it is done as a quick fix—as for an IPO, when too its efficacy is doubtful—most such communication, particularly corporate advertising, is founded on some vague notion about why and to what end it is done. Most such campaigns are stopped as they are started, for no particular reason, while other communications to various audiences carry on independently with nothing but the company's name and logo to tie them together.

Most companies that get themselves a new logo also get a whole corporate identity system that goes across everything from their stationery to signboards to delivery trucks, and then run huge campaigns announcing their new look. To be sure, a new logo and corporate identity are important to signal change, both internally and externally, but too often the logo is the only real change.

Anything done without a clear purpose is unlikely to be backed for long with management and financial resources. The moment there is a shift in priorities, or indeed a change in top management, the typical corporate campaign is aborted. No one misses it, because no one knows what it was doing for the organisation. Since no one knows whether it was working, no one can convincingly say that it deserves to be funded.

Because the company does not really have a corporate communications strategy or a plan, it also does not have the money budgeted for a corporate campaign. In a multi-division company the call goes out from the top floor for all divisions to contribute some part of their budget to a campaign that will do good to all by demonstrating the strength of the company. Once they are committed to funding the campaign, the divisions become the customers of the corporate office, which has to please all of them: and the campaign begins to be guided by that obligation in addition to, if not instead of, its original purpose—if ever one was articulated.

A typical case is ITC. Periodically its top management feel, because of some environmental pressures—stock market, regulator, activists, whatever—that despite all its diversification the company is still seen as a tobacco giant and, therefore, tarnished by all the implications of being one. The solution: run a corporate campaign to expose the other side of ITC. Predictably, that follows one of two routes—either the diversified conglomerate route, showing the range of products and services the company is engaged in; or the good citizen route, showing how the company benefits society and the economy.

The campaign peters out in a few weeks, as they typically do. Ask anyone what comes to mind when they hear the name ITC, and the top answer will be cigarettes. And the fact remains that even now cigarettes account for over 50% of ITC's revenues and over 85% of PBT.[33] It is not that there is anything fundamentally wrong with ITC: it is a well-managed company, and appears high up on every list of India's most admired and most respected companies. But, try as it might (which, for whatever reason, it periodically does), ITC can't distance itself from its core product: it is a well-regarded cigarette company, but a cigarette company it is.

## Clarity of Purpose

On the other hand, there was the UB Group.

In the late 1980s Vijay Mallya was the Chairman of a clutch of companies in the alcoholic beverages business, and was rapidly diversifying his business interests too. He was ambitious and impatient, and the funding that his companies needed to grow as fast as he wanted them to necessarily meant going public.

Mallya was the leader in both beer and spirits and had a basket of some of the most well-known brands in the country. However, because of the nature of the alcoholic beverages business, with its complex laws and tax structures, the business was comprised a myriad of companies, each of which would have to seek its own funds. Add to that his furious diversification into fields ranging from fertiliser to electronics, and Mallya saw the need to give every one of his companies a calling card: something that

33 Company website posting for year ending 31 March 2018.

would instantly give it credence for potential investors as well as employees, bankers, vendors, the trade and everyone else.

Thus was born The UB Group. With the simple expedient of tying them together with a single group identity, small and hitherto unheard of companies suddenly acquired an identity far larger than themselves. That was the single purpose of the corporate communications programme that followed: not to distance UB from alcohol, but to establish that all those companies in diverse businesses had a strong, successful group behind them.[34]

Nor was it only a bunch of ads. Back then Mallya was in the press for his social life and his interest in horses, fast cars and all of the rich boys' toys. The task of public relations was neither to quieten him down (if that was possible), nor to deny or even make up for what he did, but to leverage his personality in favour of the group. The ebullient, confident, fast-talking Vijay Mallya was the brand ambassador, his natural optimism and chutzpah reflecting on the corporate brand. By focusing on The UB Group, the name and logo were imbued with a meaning that was transferred to every company to which they were attached.

Mallya epitomised the CEO as the custodian of the corporate brand. With his innate brand sense, he was the de facto brand manager of The UB Group brand and also of Kingfisher. When he announced his plan to launch an airline and to call it Kingfisher, there was, instantly, a popular expectation of what Vijay Mallya's airline would be like. Amazingly, it was exactly that.

## Know Thyself

ANZ Grindlays was a bank that went through a tortuous history. The merger of two old British banks resulted in National Overseas and Grindlays Bank, the name later shortened to Grindlays Bank.

34 That Mallya has been in the public eye for allegations of financial irregularities in relation to his companies does not detract from the validity or the success of UB's corporate communications strategy at that time.

True to its antecedents, Grindlays was known to be *pucca*, steeped in the *boxwallah* tradition.

Citibank acquired Grindlay's in the late 1970s, found itself in a clash of civilisations, and quickly sold it to ANZ Bank, whereupon it became ANZ Grindlays. Subsequently acquired by Standard Chartered (itself a product of the merger of two old British banks, but one that had moved with the times), its business was merged with the buyer's and the Grindlays brand was, sadly, given a quiet burial.

This story, though, is just before the acquisition by Standard Chartered, in what were to be the last days of ANZ Grindlays.

In 1995 the then India CEO of ANZ Grindlays, who had been sent from London with the task of breathing life and health into the Indian operation, wanted to run a corporate advertising campaign for the bank.

When the advertising agency (Ogilvy & Mather) tried to get a brief, it was hard to get a cogent one: understandably so, because that is generally the case in corporate communications. R Sridhar, the agency's account leader on the business, had a bright idea, as he often did (and no doubt still does). At a meeting with the CEO and a few senior managers of the bank he asked, 'Over the years the bank has run several corporate campaigns. Which of those do you think best represents the bank and is closest to what you are looking for?'

Five managers had six different views, as my old boss Stanley Pinto would say, and got into a debate about what the essence of the Grindlays brand was. That was exactly what Sridhar expected, and gave him the opening he was looking for, which was to say that the first step in the process was to find out what ANZ Grindlays meant to its key constituents. Once we had a fix on that we could decide whether we wanted to reinforce it or to change it, wholly or in part.

Following the (then) Ogilvy process, we did a Brand Audit, which comprised interviews with customers and employees.

Unlike conventional market research, these are not formally structured samples. Instead, people who work on the brand do depth interviews, so that they get a first-hand experience and a feel of the nuances. The responses are then studied, sifted, sorted and a comprehensive picture of the brand (a Brand Print) is put together.

At the end of the process, after interviewing corporate customers, retail customers and employees across levels, the agency emerged with two Brand Prints: one for ANZ Grindlays; and the other, as a benchmark or a point of reference, for Citibank, the leading international bank in India. A presentation was set up, to some thirty or so senior managers of the bank.

In the weeks between the first meeting and the presentation, the bank had announced the return of the CEO to the UK and the entry of a new CEO, who was joining ANZ Grindlays after many years at Citibank. So this was going to be an interesting audience, with its three distinct segments: employees of ANZ Grindlays who made it what it was; a fireman from London who had come to change what it had become; and an incoming head coming from a culture as different as chalk from cheese.

The two brand prints, in essence, likened Citibank to a tiger—swift, aggressive, predatory—and ANZ Grindlays to an elephant (interestingly, the bank's symbol): not swift but solid, wise and sure-footed. The bank managers swelled with pride, some slightly misty-eyed, while the two CEOs looked at each other in despair: not so much at the finding, which was not a surprise, as at the pride of the managers in it!

## To Be, or Not to Be?

This led to an interesting situation, though, and one which managers of old brands often find themselves in. Whether the existing perception of Grindlays was desirable was perhaps debatable; but the clarity and consistency of that perception was not, and by that measure it had been a marvellously well-managed brand. It was what it was as a result of consistent values, policies and practices over the years, manifesting themselves in every interaction the institution had with its constituent publics, including its employees, not because of any corporate advertising campaign. What should its brand manager do: nurture, strengthen and leverage that distinctive brand? Or shed the past and change it? There is no single correct answer, but the question is a big one, and on the answer to it have hung billions of dollars in brand value.

The object of corporate marketing is, simply, to create a positive environment to do business and make profits. Positioning the corporate brand is the way for the company to determine what its stakeholders think, feel and believe about it.

## Multiple Audiences, Multiple Contact Points

What makes corporate marketing different from product marketing is the many different groups it has to reach: customers, customers' customers, employees, dealers, vendors, government, shareholders, the community at large, special interest groups... Consequently, everything about the company's operation affects its corporate marketing.

Marketing a company is in many ways like marketing a service. A product is made in a factory and is consistent from piece to piece—whether bought in a modern supermarket or at the neighbourhood *kirana* store—but a service is experienced. And because a service brand is experienced through personal interaction, not through a standard, mass-produced product, every interaction with it is unique.

Walk into a hotel. By the time you enter your room you have encountered a doorman, a receptionist and a bellboy. And by the time you check out you have also encountered a room service order taker, a room service waiter, possibly a telephone operator, a bartender, restaurant staff, a health club attendant, a cashier and perhaps a different doorman on your way out. All of them are meant to deliver—to you and to everyone else, who may encounter a totally different set of individuals—exactly the same brand. Yet in some hotels you find a consistency visit after visit and across the chain, while in others you could have a range of experiences on a single day.

The same is true of corporations. Often the same people deal with different aspects of a company: a vendor, for instance, deals with a telephone operator; various people in the procurement department; and then with the accounting department for payment. The vendor also reads newspaper reports about the company, sees its advertising, perhaps buys its products as a consumer, and perhaps buys its shares as an investor. Every interface sends a message, and too often those messages are not consistent.

A sterling example of when they are consistent has long been the Tata group, large and diversified as it is. And perhaps the single biggest factor is that its successive chairmen have walked the talk. The group's values are reflected in its every action and in the way its companies deal with their publics. If, on occasion, the interaction is not what you expect, the Tata brand is strong enough for you to treat that employee or that incident as an aberration. When, in 2016, Tata were in the news over corporate management issues and protracted boardroom battles, culminating in the contested dismissal of Cyrus Mistry, despite the unsavoury media reports many people did not know what to think. That was because to think that Ratan Tata and his supporters were in the wrong would have been to challenge strongly held beliefs and perceptions. After a period of turbulence N Chandrasekaran, the much-respected CEO of Tata Consultancy Services and long-time Tata man, was appointed chairman; life was back to normal, and it is fair to say the reputation of, and the general respect for, Tata came through the crisis undented and untarnished.

## Give a Dog a Bad Name and Hang Him

The opposite side of the coin, in many respects, is Reliance.

The biggest industrial group in India, having replaced Tata in that position a long time ago, Reliance has been known for making big, bold moves involving huge investments, high technology, complex operations, and long gestation periods, most of them successfully. Starting with synthetic textiles, the group went into backward integration into petrochemicals, then petroleum and natural gas; and diversified into telecommunications, which is now in its second avatar; retail; and media. In every one of these fields it has a major position, if not the leading one. It was Reliance which first brought the middle class into the stock market, and has rewarded shareholders well over the years. A successful business group, on all counts.

Yet the group has always had, for whatever reason, a somewhat questionable reputation. That was clearly in evidence when the Government of India announced the successful aspirants for its Institutions of Eminence programme.

In July 2018, the Ministry of Human Resource Development announced the names of six institutions of higher education—three each in the public and private sectors—that were granted the status of 'Institution of Eminence'. One of them was Jio Institute, an institution proposed to be set up by Reliance Foundation.

Immediately there was the expected hue and cry: how could an as yet non-existent institution be an Institution of Eminence? The news media were horrified. At least two eminent journalists went instantly on Twitter to question the choice of Jio. What made it worse was the provision—misinterpreted, as it turned out—that each institution would get a grant of ₹ 1,000 crore over five years.

All evidence suggests that the choice of Jio was entirely within the pre-announced framework. Besides, a company that had just posted a pre-tax profit of ₹ 36,000 crore—more than the entire turnover of all but the forty biggest companies in India—was unlikely to be bidding for a grant of ₹200 crore a year: but we don't often let facts get in the way of our perceptions.

Relevant background information and both sides of the argument are in the public domain, and are beyond the scope of the present discussion. What is of interest to us here is just this: people are quick to believe that which is consistent with their existing beliefs and biases; and, equally, to dismiss that which is not. If your company has a good reputation people will dismiss their doubts, or quickly forget the bad news; if your company has a questionable reputation people will doubt what shows it in a good light and readily believe the bad news. Perception is reality.

## The Dimensions of Image

Those who receive your communication do not distinguish company from product, ad from brochure, news report from word-of-mouth. Only marketers and their agencies do that: people at large are interested in themselves, and in what affects them. We take in the 'scraps and straws we chance upon', process them as we will, form our impressions and act accordingly.

Corporate image has three dimensions: communication, reputation and visibility. Communication is what you say about yourself; reputation is what others say about you; and visibility is sheer presence and salience. Communication, in turn, comprises that which you control, in content and delivery—like advertising—and that which you can only influence, at best—like press reports and social media posts.

The company in its image cannot be delinked from that of its products and brands. Does it make modern products or old-fashioned ones? Premium products or cheap, nasty ones? Is it in new, growing categories, or old, declining ones?

All the resulting images and impressions are related, and influence each other.

**Figure 8.2: Communications Linkages**

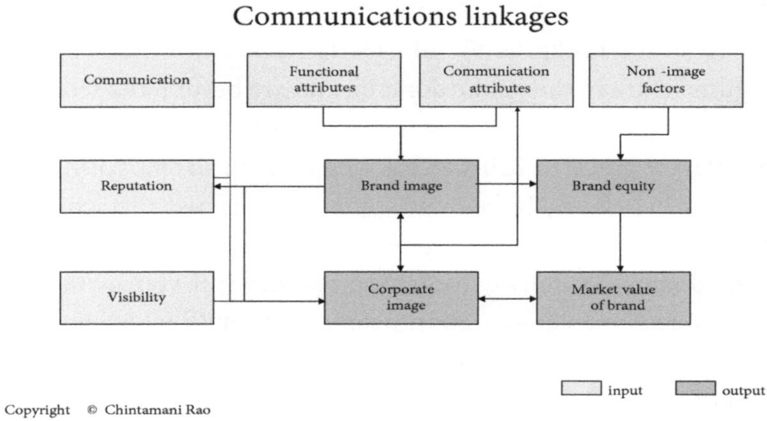


*Source*: Author

## The CEO Is the Brand Manager

While the marketing management of the company is responsible for individual products and services, the CEO is the manager of the corporate brand: the custodian of the corporate vision; the one with the authority to commit resources; and the one with the biggest stake in the outcome. That role may well be supported by specialist skills like corporate communications, but it cannot be delegated.

This role of the CEO as brand manager of the corporate brand is even bigger where a company's name is also the brand name of its products and services, like Coca-Cola or Apple or Jet Airways; or is used as a house name as in the case of Johnson & Johnson or Tata, Reliance, IBM and Sony. All the more, in such cases, everything the company says and does influences the perceptions of its customers, and the two brand spaces cannot be delinked.

'I don't know who you are.

I don't know your company.

I don't know your company's product.

I don't know what your company stands for.

I don't know your company's customers.

I don't know your company's record.

I don't know your company's reputation.

Now—what was it you wanted to sell me?'

—Text of a 1958 advertisement for
*McGraw Hill* business magazines

## The Johnson & Johnson Credo

We believe our first responsibility is to the patients, doctors and nurses, to mothers and fathers and all others who use our products and services. In meeting their needs everything we do must be of high quality. We must constantly strive to provide value, reduce our costs and maintain reasonable prices. Customers' orders must be serviced promptly and accurately. Our business partners must have an opportunity to make a fair profit.

We are responsible to our employees who work with us throughout the world. We must provide an inclusive work environment where each person must be considered as an individual. We must respect their diversity and dignity and recognize their merit. They must have a sense of security, fulfillment and purpose in their jobs. Compensation must be fair and adequate and working conditions clean, orderly and safe. We must support the health and well-being of our employees and help them fulfill their family and other personal responsibilities. Employees must feel free to make suggestions and complaints. There must be equal opportunity for employment, development and advancement for those qualified. We must provide highly capable leaders and their actions must be just and ethical.

We are responsible to the communities in which we live and work and to the world community as well. We must help people be healthier by supporting better access and care in more places around the world. We must be good citizens—support good works and charities, better health and education, and bear our fair share of taxes. We must maintain in good order the property we are privileged to use, protecting the environment and natural resources.

Our final responsibility is to our stockholders. Business must make a sound profit. We must experiment with new ideas. Research must be carried on, innovative programs developed, investments made for the future and mistakes paid for. New equipment must be purchased, new facilities provided and new products launched. Reserves must be created to provide for adverse times. When we operate according to these principles, the stockholders should realize a fair return.

— Text from company website

# CHAPTER 9
# Brand Purpose, The New Big Thing in Marketing

> **'In the purpose-addled, fake-humble world of marketing these days the only brave people are the ones pointing out what a load of bollocks brand purpose actually is.'**
>
> ***—Mark Ritson****

At the Cannes Lions Festival of Creativity in 2018, 'There was little talk of some of the seismic challenges facing those in the marketing ecosystem…but plenty of discussion about needing to make a difference,' wrote Russel Parsons in *Marketing Week*.[35] 'There are many clever people who have totally accepted that you have no hope of survival unless you can demonstrate that you are playing a positive role in people's lives, their communities, and in the world at large.'

The idea that a brand must serve a purpose larger than that of business has been around for several years, but has only recently become the subject of so much discussion. At a time when the

* Mark Ritson, 'Will Carlsberg's brave new strategy succeed? Probably', *Marketing Week*, 18 April 2019, https://www.marketingweek.com/2019/04/18/mark-ritson-carlsberg-new-strategy-succeed-probably/.

35 Russel Parsons, 'Stop mistaking purpose for differentiation,' *Marketing Week*, 3 July 2018, https://www.marketingweek.com/2018/07/03/marketers-stop-mistaking-purpose-for-differentiation/.

marketing function is in a flux, and much of the discourse on marketing forums is about justifying or defending the role of the chief marketing officer, this 'purpose-is-everything' thinking is a reflection of the zeitgeist, seeking a larger purpose for the marketing function by seeking one for the brands it serves. But where did it start?

## The Stengel 50

In 2012 Jim Stengel, former Chief Marketing Officer of Procter & Gamble, posited the thesis that brands with a purpose or ideal, a 'reason-for-being' that goes beyond the mere business motive of making profits, grow faster than their peers.[36]

Stengel first identified the fifty brands with the highest scores for loyalty, or consumer bonding, in Millward Brown's Brand Z database of 50,000. Looking for what these fifty had in common, he concluded that the X factor was a 'Brand Ideal', a shared intent by everyone in the business to improve people's lives. He then looked at the growth in share prices over ten years of the companies that owned those brands, and found that the share price of the owners of the Stengel 50, as he called them, had grown 393%, while over the same period the S&P 500 declined by 7%. In other words, the owners of the Stengel 50 outperformed the S&P 500 by 400%. Clearly, ideals were driving business growth and success.

The thesis found broad support, which was not surprising. Even without going into the data and the thinking behind it, who would argue against doing good? Over the next several years the idea gathered momentum, and became the centrepiece of marketing discourse. Indeed, some would say 2018 was the year brand purpose went mainstream.

36 Jim Stengel, *Grow: How Ideals Power Growth and Profit at the World's 50 Greatest Companies* (New York: Random House, 2012).

Research done in mid-2018 by Channel 4[37] in the UK made a case for brand purpose. Among its salient findings were the following:

1. 55% of respondents said brands should be a force for good in the world
2. 60% of young people (16 to 24-year-olds) notice ads more if they deal with important issues (55% of those aged 35–44 years; 37% of those over 45)
3. 57% of young people believe brands should use their advertising to raise awareness of social or ethical issues
4. 56% of 16 to 34-year-olds were willing to pay more for ethical products

In December 2018 Accenture released the findings of a global survey[38], reporting that 62% of customers want companies to take a stand on current and broadly relevant issues like sustainability, transparency or fair employment practices. It did say, though, that brand purpose is less important for companies producing basic, essential 'utility' products such as laundry detergent than for brands that offer an 'experience'.

Stengel's thesis seems inarguable, and later independent research seems to corroborate the desirability of brand purpose from the consumer standpoint, even if not its impact on profits. But if you look into his methodology it appears to be a case of wishful thinking.

## Wishful Thinking, Rationalised

Stengel first listed the fifty brands with the highest loyalty, or consumer bonding, scores. He then sought to determine if they

37 *Marketing for Good*, a study conducted by Hook Research for Channel 4.

38 Accenture Strategy, *From Me to We, the Rise of the Purpose-Led Brand* (August–October 2018). An online survey conducted across thirty-five countries.

were financially successful, and found that they were, which should have been no surprise. Seeking to find out what they had in common, he concluded that it was that they had high ideals. The ideals he identified for each were not the brands' stated ideals: they were what he imputed. He didn't start with brands that had declared ideals (the cause) and show that they were financially successful (the effect).

He then classified the brands into five categories, saying that the ideals of the top-performing brands centred in one of five areas of fundamental human values:

1. *Eliciting joy*: Activating experiences of happiness, wonder, and limitless possibility
2. *Enabling connection*: Enhancing the ability of people to connect with one another and the world in meaningful ways
3. *Inspiring exploration*: Helping people explore new horizons and new experiences
4. *Evoking pride*: Giving people increased confidence, strength, security, and vitality
5. *Impacting society*: Affecting society broadly, including by challenging the status quo and redefining categories

The identification of the brands with these five 'fundamental human values' is interesting. Google is in the 'Inspiring Exploration' group, never mind that Google's own stated mission is simply, 'To organise the world's information and make it universally accessible and useful.'[39] For all its undoubted success—or because of it—Google is much maligned and, because of its ubiquity and seeming omniscience, often regarded with suspicion and called

39 www.google.com/about

'the evil empire'.[40] Yes, the same Google that Stengel says owes its success to its high ideals.

Speaking of big tech and ideals, consider the case of Facebook.

After it being universally castigated; accused of everything from spying on you and selling your personal data to colluding with, or at least passively enabling, Russia to meddle in the US presidential election; and its CEO being grilled by legislatures in the US and Europe, it seems unlikely that people credit Facebook with anything in the way of high ideals. Nor is Facebook one of the Stengel 50, the world's most highly consumer-bonded brands, yet as of the third quarter of 2018 it had 2.27 billion monthly active users. Let that sink in: *30% of the world's population* use Facebook at least once a month. What's once a month, you say? Well, it had 1.5 billion *daily* active users, i.e., *nearly 20% of the world's population* use Facebook *every day.* And, no, that number was not declining in the face of all the controversy Facebook was mired in: daily active users grew from 457 million in the third quarter of 2011 to 1.5 billion in the same period of 2018—a compound annual growth rate of 18.45% over seven years, growing every single year.[41] Whatever the questions about Facebook and its integrity, they were clearly not coming in the way of people across geographies, cultures, and age buying into the brand.

And what of its financial performance? Facebook was listed on the NASDAQ on 18 May 2012. In the six years to 18 May 2018, its stock price grew by 378%, while the S&P 500 grew by 109%.[42] Whatever drove its growth, it was clearly not public perception of its ideals.

40 Being a search engine, the more Google knows, the more useful it is. Ironically, though, the more it knows, and so the better it is, the more it is regarded with suspicion and apprehension. Yet users can't seem to do without it: Google's share of search engine usage is over 90% globally.

41 Statista

42 Based on data from www.nasdaq.com.

Stengel also cites the case of Pizza Hut, though it is not on his list of 50. Pizza Hut lost its ideals in the 2000s in its chase for profit, he says. Eventually it rediscovered its lost ideals (with a little help from Stengel) and bounced back with double-digit growth as everyone concerned had a much clearer perception of what the company was trying to offer its customers. The ideal that Pizza Hut rediscovered was, 'We believe the world would be a better place if we could invest more time in relationships that are important to us, and we exist to enable and support that'.

What's wrong with Stengel's contention? Simply that the ideal Pizza Hut is meant to have rediscovered is unmanageably broad and has a tenuous relationship, at best, with its core product and service offering, which is centred on pizza. If Pizza Hut exists to make the world a better place by investing in relationships, it might just as easily diversify into greeting cards or social media.

Stengel then uses stock prices of the brands' owners to establish a causal relationship between ideals and financial success. But consider a brand like Dove (listed under the head of Impacting Society) and its possible impact on the stock price of Unilever. In 2011 the entire personal care category accounted for 33% of the company's revenue of €46.5 billion, rising to 40% of €53.7 billion in 2017. Dove is, of course, a very big brand, but of the company's portfolio of 400 it is only one of the thirteen that had sales of over €1 billion in 2017; and among the thirteen it is but one of five personal care brands.[43] Given that, it seems exceedingly unlikely that Dove as a single brand could have a measurable impact on the stock price of Unilever.

There are, similarly, several other cases in the Stengel 50—Pampers for P&G; Sensodyne for Glaxo SmithKline and Johnnie Walker for Diageo, for instance—in which the identified brand has a relatively small share in the owner company's sales, and

43 Unilever website and Wikipedia.

presumably, therefore, a relatively small impact on its financial results and stock price.

Further, having picked stock price as the indicator of success, Stengel uses the S&P 500 as the benchmark. But most of the brand owners are not listed on the NYSE or NASDAQ: many, if not most, are listed in Europe or Asia and several on other US exchanges.

If ideals do drive success, and stock price does indeed demonstrate the relationship between ideals and success, consider Nokia. One of Stengel's five fundamental human values is Enabling Connection, which includes six brands: Airtel, Blackberry, FedEx, Natura, Rakuten Ichiba and Starbucks. (Though FedEx thinks it is in the business of delivering business solutions[44], not of enabling connections.) If ever a brand was built on the thought of connecting people, it was Nokia. A perfect case, too, because the brand name was the company's name. So how did that ideal play out for Nokia? In the period in question its stock price declined by 96%.[45]

What, then, of the research, most recently by Channel 4 and Accenture, which tells us that consumers believe brands should serve a larger social purpose, and prefer those that do?

Such research is valid in so far as it asks respondents what they think and feel, and treats the finding only as what people *say* they think and feel. The problem is often with the way it is interpreted. The report says what it does. As with all market research, what you make of it and how you use it is up to you.

The Channel 4 study was a multipart effort, covering internal stakeholder, consumer and professional respondents; and combining qualitative and quantitative research and social media analysis. It was an exploratory study, examining the whole question of purpose-led advertising. To take it as

44 Company website

45 Richard Shotton, 'The Problem with Brand Purpose,' *Huffington Post*, 26 August 2017, https://www.huffingtonpost.co.uk/richard-shotton/brand-purpose_b_11679052.html?guccounter=2.

definitive or prescriptive is a mistake; and to criticise it for being what it is not, as many writers have done, is facile and counterproductive.

Coming back to what the study says, though:

1. 55% of respondents *said they agreed* with the statement that brands should be a force for good in the world. (Conversely, as many as 45% didn't.)
2. 60% of young people (16 to 24-year-olds) *claimed* that they notice ads more if they deal with important issues (55% of those 35-44 years of age; 37% of those over 45). They couldn't possibly know that they actually do.
3. 57% of young people *said* they believe brands should use their advertising to raise awareness of social or ethical issues. (Again, conversely, as many as 43% didn't.)
4. 56% of 16 to 34-year olds *said* they were willing to pay more for ethical products.

The words *said* and *claimed* are critical. As we were taught in Market Research 101, when you ask people what they do and why, they tell you what they think they do and why; or they tell you what they want you to think. This is not because they are deliberately deceptive or misleading, but because we are creatures of perception and we like to think well of ourselves, and we want to be thought well of.

## The 'Something Bigger' Trap

All too frequently these days marketers look for something that makes them look good. Nitin Paranjpe, then CEO of Hindustan Unilever, once lamented that FMCG marketers are often apologetic or defensive about what they do for a living. In twenty-first century India, where the challenges lie in technology, telecom, infrastructure and financial services, it seems frivolous, almost embarrassing, he said, for grown-ups to be engaged in peddling toothpaste, shampoo and the like.[46]

Extend that thought to the state of the world, and you can see why the desire to believe—and the need to convince private equity (PE) investors—that your company will change the world.

The trouble with the desire, and the consequent search, for a higher purpose is that it often clouds judgement and leads to self-indulgent thinking. That is what happened when Diageo thought Bailey's Irish Cream should stand for women's empowerment, with lines like 'Make Women Shine', and 'Be a Woman for Life, Not for Applause'. Women may have a marked preference for Bailey's, but what do they want from it?

'"We really believe in empowering women but people didn't want Bailey's to help them shine," [said Syl Saller, CMO of Diageo]. The brand's insight suggested that women actually wanted Bailey's to be about enjoyment, so its purpose is now: "Helping the pursuit of pleasure,"' reported Lucy Terresas in *Marketing Week*.[47] Really? Did it need research for Diageo to find out that women had Bailey's for pleasure, not because it helped them to feel empowered? The moral of the story is, don't take yourself or your brand more seriously than the consumer does.

Brand purpose is often nothing more than some lofty ideal expressed in a TV commercial and loosely linked to the category, and the only connection with the brand is that it features in the ad.

Surf Excel with '*Haar ko harao*' (Don't let defeat defeat you) is 'making people understand failure is a part of life that you need to go through to be successful. This goes back to something deeper than simple detergent powder. That is how you make a great brand,'

---

46 Nitin Paranjpe's speech at the World Marketing Congress, New Delhi, February 2011. In his characteristically gentle way, he gave a welcome reminder to all in the marketing value chain that there is more purpose to their work than they credit it with. Read more at: https://chintarao.blogspot.com/2011/03.

47 Lucy Tesseras, 'Trends for 2018: Purpose will morph back into positioning,' *Marketing Week*, 11 December 2017, https://www.marketingweek.com/2017/12/11/trends-2018-purpose-positioning/.

said Sanjiv Mehta, Chairman of Hindustan Unilever.[48] How does Surf Excel do that? By doing what detergents do: cleaning clothes. Is there anything specific Surf Excel does to that end better than or differently from other detergents? No. It's a perfectly good detergent, some might say the best, but it does nothing more than any other to help people understand that failure is a part of life.

Only a little earlier Surf Excel was telling mothers 'Dirt is good', exhorting them to 'let children blossom: play, and get dirty'.[49] A brand purpose that lasts only until the next commercial comes along cannot possibly be a rallying cry for a great brand's stakeholders.

Where does that leave us? Does it mean the notion of brands having and serving a purpose is just hot air? No, not entirely.

## Purpose by Any Other Name

Purpose, position, vision, mission: call it by any name; it is an idea that all stakeholders can rally behind, and it is more than the function served by the product or service. It's not just what you say, like a corporate tag line, though it may well be one: it is a thought, an idea that inspires, the lodestar that guides, all in the value chain who deliver the brand to its customers.

Getting back to Google, it is a sterling example of a business with a clear purpose that it pursues relentlessly and with great success. Its mission statement, 'To organise the world's information and make it universally accessible and useful', betrays no noble purpose: it doesn't speak of thereby building an empowered society or of making the world a better place in any way. Google simply does what it does: how you find that useful is up to you, be it to find a cocktail recipe or to help further your battle in the cause of environment protection. But it is clear and focused on *what* Google has set out to do, and is also not defined

48 Sanjiv Mehta, 'In Purpose We Trust', interview by Ravi Balakrishnan, *Brand Equity*, 19 September 2018.

49 Ibid.

by or limited to a specific product. Beyond Google search, 85% of the world's smartphones run on Google's Android operating system; Google Chrome has a 60% share of browsers (four times Safari at number two); many of us also use Google Maps, Gmail (1.5 billion accounts, out of 3.8 billion email accounts worldwide) and YouTube, which has become a search engine in its own right; some use Blogger, others use Google Translator, or Google Transliteration and so on.[50] Every one of these Google apps is free, as we know, and that includes the Android operating system, which is given free to mobile phone manufacturers.

Why do they give all these products away for free? For all the products and apps it has, Google is in only one business: search. The purpose of everything else is to build interaction with users. The more you use Google apps, the more Google knows about you and your interests, the more information it gathers, and the better, more customised search results it can deliver. Everything Google does is in single-minded pursuit of its mission.

Does that work for Google? In a word, yes. Its parent company Alphabet is number twenty-two on the Fortune 500, and Google's advertisement revenue accounts for over 85% of the revenue of Alphabet. And on the top three annual ranking lists of the world's most valuable brands, in 2018 it was number one on BrandZ (brand value $302 billion); number two on Interbrand ($155 billion); and number two on Forbes ($132 billion).[51]

Single-minded focus, delivering real consumer value, marketplace success and financial success are symbiotically linked, with or without nobility of purpose.

Purpose doesn't have to be lofty or about driving social change. It is called by different names—positioning for a brand, vision or mission statement for a company or, indeed, brand purpose—but what it must do is to guide the decisions and actions of everyone

50 Statista

51 Websites of Brand Z, Interbrand and Forbes

responsible for delivering the brand to its constituent markets, for a company or for a product or service. And that applies to any business, any brand, however big or small.

In the mid-1990s, Ogilvy & Mather (O&M) articulated a vision statement: 'To be the agency most valued by those who most value brands'. It was clear: O&M was not simply about creating ads; everything it did was towards understanding, being the experts on and building brands.

It wasn't just a nice set of words. I was the head of the agency's office in Mumbai and a piece of business fell into my lap. It was a mid-sized account, to release tender notices for one public sector company: full 15% commission, for doing nothing but releasing the client's text in a client-specified list of newspapers—money for nothing. I declined it. When my boss, Ranjan Kapur, heard about this he came round to my office, surprised and puzzled. 'But it has nothing to do with brands,' I said. 'You're right,' he agreed, turned around and walked away. End of discussion.

That was clarity of purpose. There was nothing lofty about it, no desire to make the world a better place: but the global management knew what kind of company it wanted to build; I, as the head of one of the hundreds of business units around the world, knew what kind of business I was expected to build; and my boss, even if surprised at first, knew that what I had done was consistent with the company's intent.

## Finding Your Purpose

If you want to do good work, or to commit some resources to putting out socially relevant messages, whatever you choose to do is valid, and better still if it has some connection with the business you are in or with what your product or service does. But the acid test of brand or business purpose is this: when it comes to making choices—in committing company resources, or hiring or firing people, or in dealing in any way with the company's many stakeholders—can the person concerned be guided by it (as I was at O&M)?

Ask anyone for an Indian example of brand purpose, and chances are they will cite Tata Tea and *Jaago Re* (*Wake up*! Or, in this context, *Awaken!*). The thought has a fairly obvious connection with tea, which (rather than coffee) is India's wake-up beverage. It began with a commercial in 2007, exhorting people to go out and vote. Since then it has gone on to address a variety of issues, such as bribery and corruption and women's rights, and has not only run ads but also actually facilitated participation in a variety of ways.

Ironically, though it is cited as an example of a lofty social purpose, it was not meant to be that. 'It is not about corporate social responsibility, it's actually a brand campaign,' said Sangeeta Talwar, then Executive Director at Tata Tea.[52] The company's website simply describes it as a cause-related marketing initiative. That places *Jaago Re* in the right perspective. If it were the brand purpose, it would have to be something a tea taster or a tea garden manager could base a choice upon.

The other—and more recent—oft-cited and much lauded instance is that of Hindustan Unilever's *Start a little good* film, exhorting people to save water. In it, a modern shower cubicle suddenly appears in a Rajasthan village. A surprised and curious villager walks in, and—contrary to an urban viewer's expectation—drinks from the shower. A long line of thirsty villagers follows, and then comes the voiceover of the protagoninst, with the message: 'Half my village drank water in the time it takes one city person to take a shower.'[53] It goes on to tell us that 'Hindustan Unilever, through its various initiatives, has managed to save 450 billion litres of water,' and urges us to 'Have a short shower. Turn off the tap. Start saving water. Help a village quench its thirst.' It also

---

52 Sangeeta Talwar quoted in 'Waking up to Brand Success,' *Forbes India*, 22 July 2009, http://www.forbesindia.com/article/breakpoint/waking-up-to-brand-success/2452/1.

53 English subtitle in the film, translated from the original Hindi voiceover.

quite virtuously informs us that the water used to shoot the film was recycled and given to the village.

The importance of water conservation is inarguable and the sentiment, as always, is laudable, but the film is liberal with the facts. As Sreekant Khandekar pointed out on LinkedIn, 'To suggest that people in rural India are short of water because of us urbanites is a travesty of the truth. According to KPMG, a staggering 89% of total water consumption in India is for irrigation. Domestic consumption (7%) and industry (4%) account for the rest. Villagers are short of water because electricity is free and farmers pump crazy amounts of sub-soil water for their fields. This is well documented. The issue is complicated, but in areas like the Indo-Gangetic plains where the water level has fallen scarily, there is a need to move away from water guzzling crops like rice. Even if we collectively resolved to bathe in two minutes flat, it would make little difference to rural India.'[54]

As the Channel 4 study says, people want to see how a brand is positively impacting the issue being addressed, and are most critical of brands that they believe are just taking advantage of a topical issue for the sake of generating good feelings. The passing statement that Hindustan Unilever has managed to save 450 billion litres of water tells us nothing meaningful. How significant is that relative to the quantity of water the company uses? Has Hindustan Unilever developed low-water detergents, so that clothes need less water to rinse? Has Hindustan Unilever addressed the issue of water pollution that detergents are known to cause? Has it taken any ground-level initiatives in the communities around its manufacturing facilities and elsewhere to help conserve water and keep it clean? If it has, we don't know that it has; if it has not, an ad hoc film is a poor substitute.

Continuing on the theme of water, Aquaguard was among the winners in the 'Effective Use of Brand Purpose' category of the 2018

54 https://www.linkedin.com/in/sreekant-khandekar-76a2719/detail/recent-activity

awards of the World Advertising Research Centre (WARC), for its *Jal Daan* initiative. Essentially, Aquaguard committed that for every pledge to give five litres of clean water on a daily basis to people in your life who need it—your domestic help, *maali*, *presswali*—Eureka Forbes would donate ₹ 10 towards installing community water purification plants for the underprivileged. The programme received high praise from the WARC awards jury for being a textbook case of brand purpose in action: addressing an issue that is socially important, with a solution that is entirely relevant to the brand, and making its purpose tangible through popular participation.

Again, WARC award notwithstanding, and laudable as it is, this is but a social service initiative. It seems unlikely that it could give guidance to a product development engineer, or to a sales manager. If it is not a touchstone for those in the brand value chain, it is not a brand purpose.

Incidentally, though, if you are not aware of the programme, you are not alone. I was not, so I checked with my social media groups, which mostly comprise marketing, advertising and media professionals. Only two people were aware of it, one a business journalist and one who had worked on it. More, its impact is unknown: neither the WARC awards report nor the website of Tandarust Bharat Foundation, under whose aegis the programme is, has that information. The Foundation's website mentions the number of awards won, but not the number of water purification plants set up; or the number of beneficiaries; or even the number of pledges made, which would at least show the amount of traction the programme has had, if not the outcome.

The starting point for finding and articulating your brand purpose has to be that it must be *grounded in reality*: of what your product or service does, and for whom. Of course it must go beyond the functional and be aspirational, but Bailey's Irish Cream thinking its purpose was to empower women was utterly divorced from its reality.

Second, it must be *something your brand or your company can deliver*, and in a manner that is distinct from, if not superior to, your competition. Google delivers on its purpose so comprehensively that there is really no need for another search engine, and that shows in its market share. In 2008, Google had a 67% share and Yahoo, 8%. Microsoft launched Bing in 2009. As of March 2019 Google had 92.5%; Yahoo, 1.8%; and Bing, 2.5%.[55] On the other hand, there is no reason to expect or to believe that Surf Excel delivers for children's growth and development; or Ariel to have men 'Share the load' with their wives; or Brooke Bond for communal harmony.

Third, the acid test: *can it guide the value chain*? 'What does the purpose mean for our business model? For our strategies? For how we recruit and develop our co-workers? What does it mean for our products and services, and for the direction in which we innovate? For production logistics? And then the external articulation—how do customers experience our purpose? Or stakeholders?' asks WARC[56], and goes on to say, 'All that's before we have even begun to think about marketing initiatives and communications. When we do start to apply purpose to these, we must be prepared to make choices if something simply doesn't fit.'

It is not as easy as making some ads.

55 http://gs.statcounter.com/search-engine-market-share#monthly-200901-201903

56 World Advertising Research Center, *Effective Use of Brand Purpose Report*, November 2018.

## CHAPTER 10

# How to Make Marketing Music

You can hear it in your head, and you know the response you want it to evoke. You must now compose and orchestrate the music: choose the instruments; think of the role each should play; and write the musical score. The wider the range of instruments available to you and the greater the distractions your audience have, the more complex your task becomes.

Back in the day when I started my career in advertising, it was all quite simple. There were daily newspapers and magazines; a commercial radio channel in each of twenty-odd cities; some 3,000 or so standalone cinemas; and hoardings, each of which was hand-painted. Doordarshan went commercial in 1976. It was, of course, in black and white, and the ads were stills that could change only every ten seconds. Every national media plan began with *The Times of India*, *Hindustan Times*, *The Statesman* and *The Hindu*. The biggest categories for advertising were FMCG like soaps, detergents and toiletries, and they too were advertised in the dailies. (I still see some and wonder why anyone would do that in the twenty-first century.)

Colour television came in 1982, as did Doordarshan's national network, and TV started to be taken seriously as an advertising medium, though Doordarshan was the sole broadcaster. In the mid-1980s, Doordarshan started to outsource programming, with what were then called sponsored programmes. It was still quite simple, though. The Hindi film on Sunday evening (Tamil film in Madras/Chennai), *Chitrahaar* on Wednesday evening (*Oliyum Oliyum* in Madras/Chennai) and *Ramayan*—later *Mahabharata*—on Sunday morning, each reached over 80% of TV-viewing homes. The rest were just fillers. Three spots a week was a good frequency. Compared with the once-in-four-weeks exposure to cinema, it was veritable bombardment.

The first National Readership Survey (NRS, the precursor of today's Indian Readership Survey) was published in 1973, but it took many years for media planning to actually start using readership data. Until then, all you had was the circulation figures of newspapers and magazines, the main ones audited but many more just what the publishers claimed.

It was a far cry from today's 800 TV channels; nearly 400 FM radio stations and 24X7 internet connectivity in over 300 million hands. Add to that the growth of PR; the plethora of event sponsorships, big and small; telemarketing; personalised mass communication via social media and email; and all of it supported with more data than anyone knows what to do with, and today's marketer has an array of seemingly unlimited possibilities.

## The Paradox of Choice

'Learning to choose is hard. Learning to choose well is harder. And learning to choose well in a world of unlimited possibilities is harder still, perhaps too hard,' as Barry Schwartz observed.[57] That is what you see playing out in marketing communications today.

Faced with a vast array of possibilities, on the one hand, and the pressure of scrutiny by corporate managements focused on quarterly financial results, on the other, risk-averse marketers stick to doing what they have always done. There is often some notion of what the 'done thing' is in a category, and if you follow

57 Barry Schwartz, *The Paradox of Choice* (New York: HarperCollins Publishers, 2005).

the herd no one will ask you why you did. And if you don't do what no one else is doing, you won't have to explain.

But in marketing there is no magic wand, no silver bullet. One size does not fit all.

In the last several years the marketing function has been wracked with self-doubt, and the CMO's role has been in question. It does seem strange that a whole functional area of management should feel so out of its depth. Consider, though, that in a rapidly changing world no function has to deal with change as much as marketing does: mainly in society and technology, with all the implications they have for how people live; what moves them; the choices available to them; what they buy and why; and the ways to reach them. In this fast-changing, increasingly complex, multipolar, multichannel world, the marketer must deal simultaneously with the strategic big picture and the minutiae of execution; make the creative leap as well as a hard-nosed justification of hard-won marketing budgets; and finally be answerable for top-line growth and brand profitability.

It's a tough job, and the response of the marketing function has been to withdraw and abdicate, rather than to gird its loins and take the challenge. When Thomas Barta asked 1,234 CMOs from seventy-four countries what they were actually responsible for[58], 77% said communications: only 39% said strategy. Note that the question was not what took most of their time: it was what they thought they were responsible for.

If communications is their main responsibility, report after report tells us that CMOs as a class are overwhelmed by the digital monster, at a loss with technology, drowning in data, and worried about data security. And more and more marketers are concerned about the lack of transparency in agency billing, rampant ad fraud in the digital space, and agencies' lack of expertise in new

58 Thomas Barta, 'What's the point of the CMO?' *Marketing Week*, 11 January 2019, https://www.marketingweek.com/2019/01/11/thomas-barta-point-cmo/?nocache=true&adfesuccess=1.

communication channels. A study by the World Federation of Advertisers[59] reports that clients give their current agency roster a score of just 5.7 out of 10, where the top score of ten is just 'fit for purpose', not exceptional or outstanding. If that seems unfair, consider that agencies themselves rate the situation slightly worse, giving the current arrangements an aggregate score of 5.2. CMOs have abdicated their strategic role and their responsibility for the top line but have little or no control over the company's data resources or technology, in which they are subservient to the CIO and the CTO.

But if marketing is uniquely complex, it is also uniquely resourced. More than any other function, it has access to a battery of external expertise. Executives at all levels routinely interact with specialists in market research, media, advertising, design, etc., whose job it is to understand consumers in their various aspects. But having a battery of in-house specialists is not enough: which one do you turn to first? If you ask the one who has only a hammer, they will see any problem as a nail.

The starting point must be an understanding of the problem or the opportunity, the barriers and triggers. What are the barriers to demand for your brand—i.e., what comes in the way of your prospects buying your brand; or buying as much or as often as you think they could? Or, what could trigger demand from non-users, or increase demand from current users? We are speaking here of communications, therefore of the barriers and triggers communications can address.

## Universal Marketing Drivers

Circa 2003 Universal McCann, the media agency of McCann Worldgroup, developed the concept of the Universal Marketing

59 Sarah Vizard, 'Trends for 2019: Agencies under attack from all sides,' *Marketing Week*, 12 December 2018, www.marketingweek.com/2018/12/12/marketing-trends-2019-agencies-under-attack/.

Drivers[60]: that, whatever you market and wherever you market it, there are seven enduring forces that drive communications success and, therefore, consumer demand. These are the seven forces, the universal marketing drivers:

1. *Brand awareness,* which means registering and keeping the brand name on people's minds. This must obviously be the starting point, the most basic requirement. Brand awareness is built primarily through mass marketing communications, but every contact point helps to build it.
2. *Emotional bond,* the sense of connection you make with your audience, beyond the functional attributes and utility of the product or service. That is what makes a product a brand; and creating, protecting and nurturing that emotional bond must be the overarching goal of all marketing communications programmes.
3. *Product news,* or creating and maintaining relevance through news and innovation; essentially, keeping the product or service fresh and relevant by developing and tweaking the offering—such as new colours and flavours; or seasonal collections of fashion brands; or facilitating purchase or use, like new same-day delivery; or a new app.
4. *Activation,* which is initiating immediate usage or purchase, creating a sense of immediacy to nudge and move the prospect from intention to action. Limited period discounts, on-pack premiums, bundled services, and end-of-season sales are typical activation measures.
5. *Loyalty,* which in this context means not a feeling—as in brand loyalty—but customer retention and repeat purchase. Airline frequent flyer programmes, hotel reward programmes and credit card points are typical

60 McCann have since stopped using this concept, at least in its original form, but a paper published in January 2005 is available at http://www.rbr.com/epaper/pdfs/CreatingDemand.pdf.

customer retention tools, but loyalty is at least as much about making customers feel wanted, with or without direct rewards.

6. *Product experience* is enabling prospects to try a product or service before they buy it. Sampling of small-ticket items is an obvious way; test-driving cars is another. The more sharply you can target your sampling the more productive it will be.
7. *Buzz* is salience: simply being seen, heard and talked about. A large part of that today is to do with the social media, where often you may neither have initiated a conversation nor have any control over it. That is, in fact, a huge preoccupation of many marketers, who feel at a loss with it, and has given rise to such questionable concepts as that you don't own the brand any more, the consumer does. That is patent nonsense: the marketer owns the brand, and it is the job of marketing to influence and channel what the consumer thinks and feels about it, as it always has been.

When you review the status of your brand, you need to ask which of these seven forces you need to enlist, to address a problem or to leverage an opportunity.

Take the instance of the India head of a well-known international brand of white goods telling me that they are competitive on every parameter, but the problem is that Samsung as a brand has a lot of buzz about it that has nothing to do with white goods. Being in mobile phones and TVs, Samsung always looks new, young and sexy. When customers go to the store, he said, that buzz carries over and Samsung is perceived as more contemporary than its white goods competitors. For Samsung that's perhaps an unplanned, unintended collateral benefit, but for its competitors it is a real issue.

If you were the head of this brand which of the seven forces would you need to harness, to address the issue? It is highly unlikely that you can make refrigerators and washing machines look young and sexy, at least not if yours is a legacy brand, so you cannot match like with like. But your brand is a white goods specialist; Samsung is not. Can you create your own buzz, leading with product news? Or should you evoke and refresh the emotional bonds that a leading, long-established brand must have, even if they are dormant?

Whichever course of action you choose, whichever forces you choose to harness, look now at the array of instruments available to you, and what do you see? A set of communication channels or disciplines: advertising, PR, social media, promotions, event sponsorship, and so on.

Which instruments you choose must depend on the task at hand. You wouldn't use a bass drum to stir romantic feelings and a xylophone wouldn't be your first choice to evoke thunder and lightning.

Likewise, any marketing driver may be influenced by several communications disciplines, but not all affect it equally; and the right disciplines have to be used in the right way. Mass media advertising is, for instance, the most effective to drive brand awareness and for forging an emotional bond, efficiently and with high reach. Public relations too will drive brand awareness, at a lower cost and often with third-party credibility, but with the limitation that you have little control over the message or where and when it is delivered. If it is buzz you need to create, public relations, events and social media are what you need.

Start by defining the task at hand. What is the issue you need to address? The answer may not be straightforward. It may call for questioning, data analysis, or even fresh market research. But if that is not clear the way ahead will not be.

Now, make two columns on a sheet of paper or on a white board. In the left-hand column list the marketing drivers; in the right, the channels of communication.

1. Which marketing drivers do you need to harness, to address the issue?
2. Which channels of communication will best influence each?

Only then do you get down to the *how* question: the messaging; the expression of the message and finally the delivery vehicles. The list of seven marketing drivers is by no means definitive. You may think some overlap; on the other hand, you may identify others. Similarly, you may, for instance, break advertising down by different roles for print and TV, or for different genres of TV.

As always in marketing, there are no right or wrong answers. What is important is the essential concept: the forces that drive demand, and how communication channels influence them. And, as always in marketing, it is not the process but how you interpret it, and what you do with it, which will make the difference.

Play on.

# About the Author

Chintamani Rao is an independent Strategic Marketing and Media Advisor. He spent nearly forty years at major global advertising agency networks, including Lintas, Ogilvy & Mather and McCann, in India and Indonesia, and in broadcasting.

As the President of Integrated Communications at McCann Worldgroup, he was responsible for managing and overseeing the agency's business in media (Universal McCann), CRM (MRM Partners), activation (Momentum), healthcare (McCann Healthcare) and public relations (Shandwick), and for pulling the agency's communications disciplines together to bear on clients' problems.

A specialist in integrated marketing communications, he has planned and led successful multi-platform campaigns for audiences ranging from upmarket business travellers to small farmers. He has advised clients on brand strategy in diverse categories, including automotive, financial services, food and beverage, healthcare, personal products, personal wear, travel and corporate brands.

Now an independent consultant, he is a noted commentator on issues in marketing and media.

www.ingramcontent.com/pod-product-compliance
Ingram Content Group UK Ltd.
Pitfield, Milton Keynes, MK11 3LW, UK
UKHW041314190726
13845UKWH00025B/264

9 789388 271721